THE FIREWALL

This edition © <u>etruscan books</u> 2006

ISBN   1 901 538 58 3 Cased
           1 901 538 57 5 Paper

Texts © Iain Sinclair 2006

<u>etruscan books</u>
28 Fowlers Court
Fore Street
Buckfastleigh
South Devonshire
ENGLAND
TQ11 0AA

etruscan@macunlimited.net
www.e-truscan.co.uk

typography: Robert Moore
printing: Athenaeum Press

THE FIREWALL

Selected Poems

1979 - 2006

Iain Sinclair

etruscan books

Contents

Introduction   7

Preface   9

Fluxions (1983)   13

Flesh Eggs & Scalp Metal (1983)   45

Autistic Poses (1985)   67

Significant Wreckage (1988)   91

Jack Elam's Other Eye (1991)   99

The Double's Double (Uncollected)   121

Penguin Modern Poets 10 (1996)   131

The Ebbing of the Kraft (1997)   155

White Goods (2002)   189

Saddling the Rabbit (2002)   215

Dead Letter Office (Uncollected)   249

Blair's Grave (2006)   259

Coming to the Crossroads (2006)   277

Index of Titles and First Lines   291

Not even The Thousand Handed Giant could easily turn over all the poems and open half of the portals of intelligence in this book. *The Firewall* is not a protective or defensive wall, it is one of the cliffs of Blake's and Coleridge's Albion sweeping against the walls of Everywhere. On this side of the waters, it spreads itself over the peaks of San Francisco with Brythonic and luminous intelligence.

Then everything changes, and we are looking at pages and worlds of rain pools, and in each one a movie ripples in its own secrecy and invisibility.

This is the landscape of another realm. We are walking over a raw and smoking surface filled with surprises. All around are the possibilities of lost tribes quietly bustling in the shadows. *The Firewall* edges towards being a world rather than paper and pages. This is a rare jewel.

Michael McClure

TRAVELLING IN SPITE STOCKINGS

'This geodesic power is the power of the JOURNEY, the successive trajectories of a moving body orientated by its locomotive power, since there is no life except within the folds...'

Paul Virilio

At a dinner table, somewhere on the fringes of Stoke Newington, I was asked what was coming next. Up to that moment, I hadn't given it any thought. 'Nothing,' I said. 'That's it.' And it was. The freebooting, casual-labouring, small press era was over. The optimism and mad energy required for texts that took years in the cooking. Allen Fisher's monumental London assemblage, *Place*, was conceived and plotted in 1970. Bill Griffiths began his assault on complacency, hurling out fragments that would, in time, if you insisted on it, cohere. His Whitechapel was gone before he reported it.

The fault line was not only visible, it was a chasm. The *Nosferatu* shadow of the She-Devil lay across the land. There would be no more poetry, no free dinners. The place where we sat would cease to be where it was. Sandringham Road, a shorthand symbol for otherworld anxiety (drugs, mugging, silver-paper trodden into the cracks in the pavement), would soon become a universal condition. With guns. In petrol stations, especially there. In fastfood outlets. Prostituted cafés and suspect cars. Bagel batteries. Small scale local fiddles rehearsing grander crimes. Hackney had always been too big, a you-are-here map in the shape of England: lights out. Time to go back to the street, the final markets and mounds.

The first Albion Village Press book, published in 1970, cost around £50. The last, in 1979, left me owing £2,000. Money which would be paid off, inch by sorry inch, through years on the road, bookdealing. The candle of ego flickered and went out, the courage. Who would be interested, now, in language sermons, spiked satires, dull-witted subversion of Blakean rhetoric? If possession doesn't *take* the word dies on the page. The potential readership, fellow poets, were otherwise engaged with their own strategies of survival: reinvention or grateful disappearance.

Douglas Oliver, in a letter which took me seven years to answer, by way of a novel, said: 'We live a news story and enter its present state affected by event and mood: a phantasmic world does arise, is appropriate and exact, is even phenomenal for us, rather as a ghost would be. Here, there's a crucial difference between bad poets and good. Any fool can know about these things by reading about them; any fool can construct surrealistic or fantastic visions, and, having worked them out, can even see them. But the good poet, working in such fields of knowing, doesn't necessarily "want" to see what he sees; he just sees it, impelled necessarily upon him by circumstance and mood and by his trust in those, his willingness to speak whether gripped by horrors or by beatitudes or by some kind of common-sense.'

The grip of necessity had slackened. I thought Doug was talking, with care, about what was done with, over, discriminations of ancient darkness. History. His Story. But he was describing, I see now, what was coming next. News that blackened the whites of your eyes. Poison that invaded your pores. Sour air that sickened the mouth.

So the agreement was this, to become a bad poet, to start again, from zero. Learning, painfully, to put one line after another. Writing from a notional centre, the floating Gothic principality of Whitechapel/Limehouse, was no longer permitted. The circumference, as Virilio suggests, is everywhere and the centre nowhere. Language pinched, imagination constricted; not many counters in the hand. *Heat. Glass. Air. Night. Stone.* That audience, edgy but generous, waiting their turn at the lectern, had dispersed, bunkered down. No more performance rants, no punk Vorticism.

For years, I was not at home; out there, on the move, neurotically restless, trawling for stock. I never kept diaries or journals. I stopped making 8mm films when the cameras gave up the ghost. There were no photographs. Short texts, barely poems at all, were unfranked postcard notations: there was nobody to send them to and they had very little to say. Reading these things back, I remember: internal strain, external pressure. Unease ameliorated by scratching a few words - difficult to transcribe - on scraps of paper. Three booklets, produced in smaller and smaller editions (21 copies, 12 copies, 10 copies), were instant printed (like a secondhand book catalogue), then given away. No takers, no come back. The right response. (With the trade lists, the phone started ringing at 6.30AM. Signifying two things: that the postal system, in parts of England, was still operative and efficient. And, secondly, that we were all deeply implicated in the free market, scuffling, selling. Cash as the only reality. A quaint notion carrying dire consequences.)

As we limped from one form of conservatism to a worse, surviving poets were dosed on hot sweet tea, dusted down and invisibly published. I seemed to do most of my writing in post offices (just before they vanished). The queue was the urban narrative: much dealing (fake cigarettes packed with sawdust, wraps and knock-offs) took place in this zone, where time stretched like cuckoo-spit. There were generous viral exchanges. You could try every kind of exotic import: bird flu from China, malaria from the tropics, Balkan shivers. The deal that never took was between the expelled Kenyan Asian countermen, behind fractured glass, and the over-impatient Afro-Caribbean clients who needed to be elsewhere, with bundles of inadequate documentation. Every few months the whole business would be closed down for another police investigation.

I recover my sense of London from these coded fragments in a way that more considered prose pieces, fiction or essay, won't allow. Child abuse scandals of bureaucratic arrogance, incompetence: an overwhelmed exhaustion of means. Saturation policing when there is camera drama or the unpoliced mundane of muggings and car crime. The rubbish on the streets, once picked over, recycled for profit, is now a mess of spilling green eco-bins, rats and pigeons. There are squirrels in the eaves. Throwaway poems, the looser the better, are quietly prophetic. I don't want to give nostalgia a good press, but unframed, uncrimped effusions call up corners of lost worlds that are still usefully remembered. I can see where the more public books, their front, their faked omnipotence, come from. Poems are factored out of future novels, aborted films: the same landscape, the same weather. No characters need to be invented to manufacture drama or consoling authorial whispers.

The politics are unsafe, the theory fraudulent. If it's not lived experience, it's not in the movie. Cinema and its bastard off-spring, television, is the addiction, always: unanchored imagery, analgesic colours. They were the double lives I wanted most, film and poetry. These tight-lipped scripts are about not getting them. And about the world, its tender body, as a consolation.

FLUXIONS
(1983)

'I remember he told me, she sent him to a famous Apothecary for some Unicornes-horne, which he resolved to try with a spider which he incircled in it, but without the expected successe; the spider would goe over, and through and through, unconcerned.'

ROUGH TRADES (*OAKHAM*)

smalltown mid-land
moults to green

which is history is
a defeated grey lumen

lichenous crust becoming
stone-flesh

finger forced down
the dragon's throat

armed church loses height
old man deflated

there is a place to approach
a closer place to stand

moisture in loose air
it clings to the citizens

& how many angels dance
on the head of a nail

driven hard through
the eye of a needle

THE GLAMOUR'S OFF

the epic which is a tractor
with hay bales, turning
righthand margin
of a middle english field

propaganda displacement of
such heroic proportion

chlorine in the urinal
- Northampton - hissing
of childhood vanishing

diamonds-in-glass & violet
necropolis light
the expulsion of bottled guinness

what he can use, he does

THE FALLS (*TALGARTH*)

we are not given many and do not realise
instants set quick out of darkening air

rainladen sky burns off
the tree's plump skirt

horsemen appear and disappear in the night
witnessed the human town comes alive

trapped stars of whisky sulphur
caught in thermals

we have fucked out holes in the black foliage

bodybreath, curtains open
shadows across

where the pigs are dragged
in view of
our fascinated children

imprint of entwined bodies, such glad heat
& then the knife the screams the meaning

FLUXIONS (*LINCOLN*)

As in a story...

over the plain the citadel
earth & water, night
interwoven in us, elements
of smelt & folded darkness

en train, behind our motives
'we're on the edge'

fog'd headlamps beam the stone,
salt-fired windows;
lights fanned into misty rain

'His red eyes again! They are the same!'

ruffled furrowed bitten slippery
mucoid itch, soil detonated
between dung & flower, slithering
tongue stitched at both ends, wet

sheets enclosing us
'invoiced as clay'

(now) standing inside the intention
and seeing it, whole

De Mote Corporum

RED HAIR, LIKE A SPIDER GLUTTED ON IRON

spent in
Lamian transactions

lovesdeath
the sea-house

bloody
mouth

wool & water: the bite
of implacable insects

beneath desire
and its increments

underinflamed, over-informed
insulting the vegetable lattice

wave drawn into bow
desiccated vibration

queer curdled water

WRITTEN AT ATTENTION, TO THE SOUND OF RUNNING WATER (*LONDON ZOO*)

Ophitic spit: mention another
writer and I'll split your cleft,
stick one on your spine,
salmon & ball, weapon snatched
out of imagination, full snake
stuffed with broken concrete

how like a turtle
is the photographed head
of Ronald Reagan

threat colours the road, our map
is animated by a pulse of emotion;
old men dry as sticks made ready
for holy fire, hell is frozen
for the Christmas skating waltz,
camels shit as they spin

weather of

teeth loose in gum, fern-prints
in dirty Camden snow

DROWNED FIELDS (*WHITECHAPEL*)

Fire or an angled wind
snowbough graved to earth

ahead, half-light's crystal
sparking the crust

'catastrophe' sealed within
my brain's frozen apartments

rubble disappears
memory released

tender ghetto histories
dignify sleepwalkers

'the edges of the abyss'
sustains illusion

& shutters
a faltering transcription

ENTERING COLIN COUNTRY (*BEYOND STAMFORD*)

hearing the approach of fish
the grinding of their teeth

through the trepanned dome
of cloud-country vapours
the road swoons in pulse
regulated by forks of trees
bending from our unfocused velocity

a wiseblood preacher outside railings
of a Church-for-Sale spittles
his congregation with glottal rant,
the uncorrected slip of
'resent' for 'relent': utter damnation
best hope among snail-horn steeples

2

one breath later a roadside pub
sunk in fens where gothick poverty
fed the English opium crop:
the moon-faced idiocy of dazed mechanicals
watching their entrails turn to water
high on turnips
rotting in black overloam'd mud

Arabs, according to the *Guardian*, hit Warsaw
for cheap prostitutes and wholesale ordnance

'You used to keep cigars you know
the ones rolled from adobe'

some days we take on more of the surface
than we can handle
this whole wide zone
is a plate nobody can swallow

try Boston, Lincs, for an evolutionary fix
what might growling
have crawled out of river silt

XENOMANIA, THE ROAD

for Driffield

above

darkened water, above the...

from deep outside,
a mercury bulb,
filament burning, news-speak

sleepless, livid harbour
dream of deadman's suit & failure
holding the table down
with the weight of our elbows;
eyehair flexes in convulsion,
concentration concentrates around
ring of slack muscle, an icepick'd
fish served up, serves you right

always the machine hormone
bent by starwave
'damn vegetable verse & double-
damn vegetable philosophy'
unaccustomed regularity in the ionosphere
notebook: as tool
ethics of refinement, price of tin

'the air is different here'

2

fear of the dog, clinging also
black imitation silk, woman
assets stripped, empty shelves

green fettuccine, discussing
Suicide & Envy,
which he splits, rigorously,
from Jealousy, condemning again
the OED's lack of a firm line

Timaeus: 'What God is / the absence of envy'

3

out of the claypit white
responsibility for under-
redeemed speculator's desire for
what he accepts & most fears

Houdini dislocated his arm
that the magic be successful
saw the drowned joining hands
& rising into present time

at whose mercy...
'moulting pudenda'...
through uncalibrated space, we
follow the lure of dolphins

'SERVED CLUMSILY' (*TOTNES*)

Dartington territory, fine bright air
lit fields in coming waves

of their own protection:
anoraks are fresh and unhorsed

enter, distracted, novel in pocket
brown rice in turn-ups, a husband

'Buy the cow's yogurt and tell him
it's goat. He'll never
know the difference'

these couples can't quarrel
by anything but implication

clean clean clean; yawning
to the borders of Babylon

APPROACHING OUNDLE BY ROAD

here and there
squares of yellow rape

extinguish malpractice
sunset to full-steam

watertower rising over
the rising rim

coming to it on balding tyres
you are the straight course

CROSSING THE MORNING (*VALE CRUCIS*)

climbing sun boulders the hillcrest
between stones a cat appears
ingratiating or tactical, completing
the arc & arrow of low-rolled desire

chopped pillars make an altar or anvil

here the feather the ant
does its work
versing and reversing, willing its will
a system of hair-fine lines;
by its direct movements, abrupt to the eye
its blade its balance
making this place, whole

all those branches, windows, archways
water-chest open to new air
leaf-drenched dark pools, unmeditated
fold back to the river and the hills

kingstone set apart
on ground that pulses like a warning

that stands because the rest has fallen

CRYING, LIFE! LIFE! (*TOWARDS BEDFORD*)

furze warmed
where hare is absent

landscape without risk
contained

wind-shifts &
animals bruise verges

black to green
to blue to grey

'shimmering' distance
velveteen moss

the recorder records
no other function

or desire

DOCTRINE OF VARNISHED MORTAR

Nether Stowey
      to Highgate

Coleridge's aching head
          my gums

Quantock ridge in smudge of sun

stacked sheep
      the altitude

damp like car wash, *rinse please*

pain converted
      nerves silent

MORPHIC RESONANCE

wasps mate with shadows,
sun of the east through vapour,
the best time, mellow brick,
yolk of egg prematurely aborted

nesting active where
old wood weathers under
tired guttering, our
thunder-coloured slates

grasping grasping ...
struck down by pale straw
'my name's Patrick Golden,
I've been stung by a bee'

COMBUSTIBLE STONES

'By means of a sympathetic powder which he imagined he had discovered: this powder was to be rubbed on the weapon causing the wound, not the wound itself.'

A HANDSHAKE ON THE TELEPHONE

'Dreams are descriptions of how things REALLY are. They are accurate.
As real as a car smashing a cat in thee road.'
                                        Genesis P-Orridge

if the cat has your name and dies
consciousness extinguished on a wheel
spun against railings you do not
die of it or lose one single life

the figure at the window removes
his shadow falls back from glass
the smear remains and stays
cat's eye within his eye
polishing detonations of sunlight

and where the beams cross
an accident awaits the supplicant

who slides from flowerbed to shower
limping after a dole of
pumice bread and a wafer
that makes the tongue its target

contours already wind back
like the tongues of spiders

thinking of what the ghosts told me
and why and why
temperature changes in my belly

remembering a taste, heart in hand
a drawer bending towards sawdust

they have made the staircase
a metaphor to be respected

FEINT, DUPLICATE, CHALLENGE

WHITE AIR

'Glue Sniffing Kills. We do not sell glue to anyone under 16.'

Jersey Airport.

the figure of the messenger
'congestion of the lungs'

eyes fixed beyond answer
no strings to his bow

which therefore becomes
more than a weapon

two suns in taxi window
without heart, no language

so forget this attempt
to define 'The Primitive'

no use in knees either
crawling or lying on the ground

the moon is not a sentence
but a clear sign

worn on the forehead
of a universal mystery

the sea a solid
undisturbed by vehicles

when you've finished laundering money
the dirt has to stick somewhere

ropes of smoke
hanging & breaking in motion

a stillness so perfect
we think of dying

and risk saying so

RE-READING *ROTHSCHILD'S LAPWING*

some things the same
some different

Augustus John took out his cock
& laid it on the desktop like a ruler

for females in hats to admire
or fondle in revulsion

two christian names
do not make a christian

RADIO STRUMPETS

tonight, albumen, the moon
is better understood than earth

leafless poles mistaken
for suiciding whales

hurl themselves
on Lincolnshire mudflats

car radio *Archers* rhyme
'lesion' with 'Martian'

& more locally:
'Genesis is Missing'

KITING THE FLIES

always the muff, mouth agape
stealing fond bacteria

this field a cold ghost
excising the ecliptic

pacing the chrism
on highheel blisters

from Myrdle Court out:
nothing

in goes the gelt
thudding paper

silencing the disease
of white domestic business

A SUITCASE CALLED ANTLER

earlier when

finger tips / going west
pads throbbing wellbeing
faces in pads
pads whirling like drills

attention, rapidly reading
or being read to
'the sedes stercorata or pierced chair,
and its possible use for
making absolutely certain of the sex
a newly elected Pope'

Milton. Life. His window
the entire phallus of thought
(like basalt, he said)
George Dance's columns, symmetry
against Hawksmoor's fossil force

the west gate of Bunhill Fields
locked, wife
taking my daughter to witness
death placards of non-
conformers, dissenting skeletons

this is / not what I set out to talk about

2

on the platform Liverpool Street
Central Line train
pulling away a friend's wife
another man's arm intimate
laughter did not speak
of who or what
but to now report
in terms quite distinct from
those originally considered

tiled corridor runs uphill
to the right the end
which could be directly into a wall

'it won't bite'

illicit lovers in balance
woolly coats
growing still
the backs of urban sheep

FLESH EGGS & SCALP METAL
(1983)

'Everything is verboten... that isn't obligatory.'
Francis Stuart

CASTING DEVILS AS SHELLFISH

in midair shifting gravity to open doors
scribbling and sliding cards or tabulations
novelty comes in the form of bills, two colour
print jobs with red dominant; beneath these
fictional climaxes gulls or grays swoop
smoother than memory, from the west
my strong right hand all that's lost before

a gold watch laid out its owner buried
a box in earth and probably now
decayed into gas, caved in, so that ribs
are stones but no burden no will
to make of them a new-minted woman

as the food motive fades dusty coffee
peels nerve to irritating edge
conversation divided into drink and criticism

I still believe the river is a medium
terror ceases when the human
voice is quieted or stopped
by the roar of plants choking

earth-organ / turned coat

wanting to say it but not to you

SPIRIT LEVELS

'The wish comes/ to write about the places/ I have come to'

The hills above Port Glasgow
the most impressive the stopped
hierarchies of Azrael,
not yet hoarded and ash-scattered
in Cricklewood: unrisen sons
and the air... rich as bovril

on Hillhead the buildings -
it's the broken English aristos who
need the malt, Jimmie,
and lamb-knuckle tikka
is dished in accents of impure
Jock Stein. They're pillaging
stored dust, *Voltaire & Rousseau*

whose mouth opens to the ice-
ocean, Polaris
grounded, resurrection blasts locks
from monuments, multitudes
of vertical corpses, capital of dolour

under rain-stones
the dead sleep, face downwards

the beauty of
slums built to last a thousand years,
a Reich of greyblue blocks;
no better skyline in Europe
no better place to view
than from under

o lovely / gash of truth

BATTERIES OR WHISKY

'You could hear rats piss on cotton'
                                    Charlie Parker

In Victoria's Park...

police exercise their dogs &
gangsters their imagination

in sweated nylon jumpsuits
the narcissism of pumped muscle

'always good for a ruck'

...the petting of wolves

HOME OF THE TONG, OR
THE DREAM-DETECTIVE

'he had mistaken the sheep in question for a WREN wearing a
sheepskin coat'

inside: sheep
outside: people

west wind draws us
the entrails of a rabbit

a low-flying owl
against the Tor's resistance

LA RAGE (*PENZANCE*)

7 hours sealed, hurtling or snoring
fingerprints & daggers of black hair

schlepping tides, harbour waves
roll like a pregnancy

searchlight parts brown clouds
to Michael's mounted nipple

rubber gloves & worm powders
active to the last gramme

A BULL CALLED REMORSE

either nude and shoved behind as well as
fixed in plucking mud, anchor
to his own need, as the Silurian effluent
scums to the surface
in a vortex of jaw-defying squidmeat

'elegant' says the child, meaning the opposite
and accurate to the last spasm

scraping sunwounds from salmon
adrenalin releasing warts
of dried mushroom a flashback
filmdeath, dyed in the Sixties,
red paint hair / the tribesman cannot
write himself back into his former clan

inactive in a wholly alien period, he finds
the lock that his special interest deformity
can access: he is alone and singular

all hooks out, defenceless
two salt channels of information
pitting tangerine cheeks

with Madame Thatcher
'I've had to learn to carve meat'

HENCE, LIKE FOXES

as unlikely as 'Canadian Pataphysics'
heat, a lovely block word
that can so easily be placed alongside
simple terms such as 'Big' or 'White'
and impersonated by Lee Marvin or
a robot version, less complicated
more enthusiastic than the original

guardian 'po-lice' with faces
like their helmets hotwire generic Rovers
(the colour of dogsick), haul 'em off
spray-shirted, chisel-peak hair, built
around ginger moustaches, quiet fans
of the simplest solution, polishing
our kidneys with their soft boots

riotous streets out of control when a
hi-definition lo-rent blonde is hallucinated
without underwear, by a stoop of panting
stationer's assistants, a smoking
shamrock lounge of horseflesh punters

all sublimate erections into truncheons
and back again, streetlife gets
stickier by the hour (Sandringham Road)

longing for darkness when the blunted leaves
split and spill their poultice of black juices
and we dream of travelling oaks
freedom to move in the excrement of birds

BIG FACE, SMALL RAZOR

seaweed luxury bath essence
the same colour as

Luis Buñuel's *Last Breath*
in uncorrected proof form

to be read (solo) in water
cooler than blood: relished

domestic in affections and
without pretence, shocking

like a child's skirt
lifted by a blindman's stick

avoid the doctrinaire blue/grey of
Coronation Street's latest transfusion

or cast a 20-million-dollar investment
around the skin tone of an 8ft mammal

wild light denting water, blinding
the bland in blue suspension

FLESH EGGS (*TRELIGGA*)

white herm: a cyclone
of sticky dust
expressing no relief

as rods in their circuit
grind small wind, water-
wheel set in baked earth

the magnetic west weakens
stomach and prose
letting in too much 'nature'

grateful then for the timidity of sheep
but surprised when one nips your flesh
with pastry-cutting teeth: 'what kind

are the rocks?' no kind. shattering
drench of spray resolved waves
unscrew themselves in a bravado

like genocide, too baroque a rhetoric
for the Spanish maestro, the deaf one
the losers say: 'shut up and deal!'

A FEW HUNDRED YARDS FROM
THE DWELLING OF MR PRYNNE

under slow-flume
a net of pubic mosses

'The Fort Saint George in England'
is overall workers

plane trees
guinness bottles

sculls, flat to water
spindle-oared

sweating off meat
as we must

fossil evidence
of a diminishing future

Excelsior!

I dip my left hand
into Cambridge river

POST-RABBINICAL SLUMBERS

fixed fallen folded / dereliction
within and beyond the mesh

unmoved unmoving
pieces of the circumference of a clock

held in the lock of inertia
whitesick grass the surge

a spittled challenge:
Ahhr Gütten Whurr Shah

having the weight of tribal allusion
archaic industrial slaughter-pens

a hugely deformed condom
like a rubber support stocking

but there is, equally, another story
the heroine rising at night

to sheath chairlegs
in pristine french letters

a joy image, a generative dance
scratch on heart made silent

MORE AMOROUS THAN IMAGINATIVE

there was a man set to dig a stone
from earth, a woman's promise
to give her body, openly & immediately
upon its successful removal

he took off his wristwatch, wanting
no local & irritating
sense of time, he also
abandoned his spectacles

work continued, with little progress
for two days, nights spoiled with
contradictory dreams: post-industrial
landscapes, ugly future roadsides

& when the stone finally yielded
wearied of labour he went into
the woman, not needing her now
tight with what he had expended

so much he could in no way
avail himself, nevertheless
he did, hugely, rid of the desire
to speak more of this sorry matter

GERMAN BITE

for Gerry Goldstein

an excitement of too much

the hands of the junkie not as
spectacular as the hands of Orlac
but as much of a functioning instrument
guiding the hit into what's left of
the thinking machine

as if talking could be anything more than talking
the world unsettled and not remade

too many reports of books telephones visions
explaining the Usury Theory while
eagerly demonstrating it

blood under the skin & paper-dirt on it

NOSTALGIA IS A WEAPON LIKE
THE BLISS OF PETER RACHMAN

'The jacket he wore on only a few subsequent occasions,
the last being his funeral.'

a warren of secrets
undemolished
and undemonstrated

sour to ease pain
scent-cushioned
lap of poodle: poodle cup

halter on judge's bulge neck,
slack-corseted to drag
the sledge of respect

2

after hours, by manufactured
candlelight, his wrestler
glistens: vaseline buffalo

sold cheap as brick
(£1 securing two houses), or:
bitten off and swallowed

like the spade pimp's tongue:
who minds this
puts it far from reach

3

vulcanise old wrongs
to plate new,
yesterday's whore mother

today's victim who
gilds the chain
attaches a German shepherd

to the trunk of his keeper
and remember please
money pays for this page too

4

so offer your screenplay to
the late
Rainer Werner Fassbinder

TALKING WITH CAROLYN

'I am starting sax lessons in September... Psychoanalysis
follows in October.'
        Neal Cassady

        dusted in unexceptional manuscripts
        the truth that was and is now

        an over-applied cosmetic
        eyelashes cut from flea-combs

        still capable, on parting, a touch
        ring hand to shoulder

        comrades in a revolution
        that had been decisively defeated

        talking with our brains cut out
        shocked to be lifted

        from the safety of myth

A HAT THROWN IN THE AIR, A LEG THAT'S LOST

'An honest woman breaks her leg at home.'
                                    Luis Buñuel

trust is a meadow the light in my eyes
a peculiar opacity, fearing blindness
and surprise itself, the source of fear

honouring the mortar the ditch
in photographs that remain potential:
whistle of an arrow or bark of a dog

hearing in images the ear has a greater
depth of field and what it cannot fix
goes back into the borders of darkness

better to exercise your fingers
across the tabletop
than mutilate a sonata

dream is serial like *The Vengeance of Fu Manchu*,
each sequence having the same
weight and structure, a pornography

of gesture not action, asleep in the chair
but not yet become it, solitude lacquers
wax fruit in a golden bowl

AUTISTIC POSES
(1985)

STREET DETAIL

his bare arm, a gold box
on the roof of the red Jag

at the lights and then
having to flick the box

into the street not
breaking off his talk

FOR SALE notice
phone number on ledge

you don't stuff the packet back
through a window of that vintage

old-style smoking villains

LOWESTOFT TWINNED WITH PLAISIR

an old man cycling
basket of mouldy sprouts

collie peeing in gateway
steaming pools
glisten in a prophylactic sun

traffic held while
grey merchantman glides
up the fast lane

-fast?

novels have been written
waiting for East Anglian
bookshops to open

WARD BONDAGE

talking of the Sheik, his rivers of blood speech
foul papers passed to the DPP

'Look it up in the phone book & write
a Dear Sir It Has Come To My Notice And I Feel
It My Duty letter. Leave it to them'

local politics: chewing garlic buttons
under striplighting in a green kitchen

Muslims to the East, Ashkenazim to North;
the West Africans won't get involved

'It's not the money. 25 grand's
a bagatelle, we can lose that in petty cash'

the cat asleep on manure pile's straw
loamy soil of former market garden

in Hoxton the Turks call themselves black
thinking of the holes in your stockings

a mild & glittering nightwalk home

TO WHOM IT MAY CONCERN

Dear Sir/Madam,

I act on behalf of a client who has been charged with offences of robbery under the Theft Act and of offences involving firearms under the Firearms Act. He has been committed to the Central Criminal Court to stand his trial.

The allegation concerns what amounts to an attempt to rob with the use of firearms, a Securicor van which was making a delivery and/or collection at the school in Albion Drive E8 on the 30th November 1984 shortly after 10AM.

I understand from my client and other sources that civilian witnesses from nearby houses may well have come on to the street once the Police operation to arrest certain persons at the scene commenced. I wish to take statements from any witnesses to the incident and if you were such a witness I shall be grateful if you would telephone me on the above number so that we can arrange a convenient time and place to meet.

I confirm that any enquiries will be treated in the strictest confidence.

tanking in behind screams the
padded jackets bomb all pale
drumming soft ribs/ nervepitch
white & dry with unvoided sick

hot wheels slaughter the domestic
invisible to their limp
but dirty shoes/ the TomTom
sports a fine tan, bottle's gone

cuffs bite, mistake mood,
flagcars scrape/ the old blue
pull out, back to the nick, fitted
to fleece: nice try, lick tar

shooter swinging from finger,
postcoital disuse
YR FUCKIN DEAD SON/ wait
for light to change, temper-

ature/ count heads for collar,
odds are even (4/1) TEAR
HIS NUTS OFF, car boot
empty as grave, they pose

camera snaps not
the scene the crime but
this grin team, frame
out plods/ horror

fellaheen sees vision
of his hell with
plenty more to follow, slap'd
in the runabout, then

the hole: technical bits
come after
thick chains & rolled-up
sleeves/ day of

water-sun, spiked balls
hanging in winter trees/
a fence beyond
venal streaks of news

AUTISTIC POSES

'alive, but past recall'

her heels worn raw
two bacon-coloured patches
dollar-sized

black crombie,
collar turned up &
covered in white doghair

'I haven't been well'

damp snuffling ahead,
dry rasping cough behind

the shopping precinct
disappears into a glass screen:

THIS SAFE HAS A TIME DELAYING LOCK

our official, no brahmin,
low caste as an umpire,
shovels out reluctant benefits

on his wall a map of London
cut off at the Thames

the South is not simply *terra incognita*
it doesn't exist

SERPENT TO ZYMURGY

more diseases than textbooks

I had thought St. Vitus's dance as
much a back number as the cakewalk,
it's stomping here in full fig,
velveteen jacket worn to flesh, pocket
torn out like a split cheekbone

try and lift from the coop of
Old Holborn, phlegm, twitchy
parrot moods: they've even picked up
on bird diseases and foul pests

the lolling sheepheaded beaten
men, the form-filling
dole-scratching, ill-tempered
lumpen mess of what we are become

this post office has more patients
than a surgery, sliding to
the taped window across
a gob-spattered stone floor

on the low wall of the flats
a girl perfectly imitates the
ka-aar of the shit-eating seagull

ka-aar, ka-aar, ka-aar
wait long enough / & nothing changes

AN IRISH NOVELLA

'Be a waiter.'
   W.S. Burroughs to Carl Solomon

Shadows across the desk were obtrusively dense, the detail too interesting. And more real than the rest of the furniture - which can be rapidly sketched, plywood suggesting a safe or closet in which to change the changes of clothing he didn't have.

Heat outside, no sun. Pan make-up drying natural sweat. The overhead fan offered no relief, a cutaway. He didn't move and there were no lines for him to say.

Somebody wanted something, a girl. Grey hair the colour of a drained washbasin in a station hotel. Grey skin with fatty dots in it, globes of misinformation. She was *A Few of Kiki's Beautiful Friends.* And she wanted something. She wanted to discover a valid use for the first person singular in a terse narrative. A use that would not involve compromise.

The problem was without solution. If he took the case he was finished. He would thin to an identity crisis. If the brothers found out he would require an immediate retread. He'd have the feds from back east camping in his rear view mirror.

Lear in Japanese is Chaos. Is *Ran.* Daughters are sons. The Fool dresses like a woman.

What if Kiki's Friend was a man? And not a Few?

Hard to get out from under. Cigarettes are punctuation, prohibitively anachronistic. Brandy is a wine. He held the tooth glass up to the light. A single bulb. There were prints all around the rim. Of lips, not teeth. And not his own.

I can crack this case, he thought. The foxy lady couldn't run. She was wearing a stiff's weight in dead skins. He couldn't move either. But he could disappear.

In another life, some damaged citizens helped to empty empty bottles. Risk-takers unaware of their crust. The barman poured spirits through open hands, newspaper funnels.

There was one other thing. A small book in a large pocket. It stayed shut, brittle edges of yellow paper flaking to a dust that slowly filled the hungry darkness. If he could switch coats he could switch stories. And that might be for the best.

'They were coming toward him,' said the Chinaman, 'and toward no one else.'

14 DIE IN TREE FEUD

an unclarified moon bounces
how well it describes itself

or the boat of anguish starts
from Max von Sydow's teeth

scalded with cold the night
sun in our nail also rises

nacreous
& at a fixed distance

the bole of this london plane
feels the dark by opposing it

in our contraries more
sensibility than sense

'that love, call'd Friendship'

DYNASTY = NASTY YAWN

'There are fish whose body temperature is so low
they die when touched by the warmth of a human hand'

as to the clinker'd heart -
the curvature of time is true!

the bacon you smelled at 9AM
we ate at one

snow slips in a dagger
from our daughter's nose

WHARF WHARF

'the lee side of a sewer'

in Madison the squares
tend their own garden

songbirds, informers
& Ritz Marxists

Marlon's blind cab
is bolted to the floor

'contender'
'been'

'some'
'Charlie'

journey to the end of
nowhere, a coldstore

fat pockets, cigar stick
unemployed dynamite

paintstripper, bro'
requires no chaser

GOOD ICE: DO NOT ENTER THROUGH RUBBER DOORS

'Washing hair or clothes often just produces cleaner lice'

'Ain't got much expenses,' Eddie said. Man without expenses is nothing. We are the sum of our expenses, thought Feather. Morris didn't need to think it: catch that haircut, the over-compensating jockey shorts, suspenders keeping folds out of his stockings.

You can't kill a man without expenses. And. You can't kill, a man without expenses. The gun looked stupid. A piece taken from some larger and more effective machine. It looked like a starting handle with nothing to start.

Eddie felt the awful letdown of the camera moving away from mirror to man. He was that man. Who then had been inside the mirror? A catatonic depression spread heavy shadows. Chilled light striped a stubble-textured jaw. He sagged over the half-live burger. Blood or ketchup? Cardboard shoes. Wet feet. Snow in summer. Night for day. A forgotten bill. An unlocked automobile. A friendly witness in an empty window.

Feather couldn't talk to a man who had butter sliding off his coat. Dried snot you want to pick from a stranger's nostril.

If you could teach the car to shoot you'd cut out the middleman, thought Morris. And the expenses, added Feather, working up an act, reading his own mind.

THOSE TIMES

Cocteau directing
La Belle et La Bête

'suffered so badly from eczema
that he had to work with
a black cotton mask over his face'

outside the studio,
a constant
'roar of planes'

the same city
now features
a parade of prostitutes

cloth butterflies
covering furious eyes

DETAILED DESCRIPTION OF A HOMOSEXUAL ACT

'Two of them named Ron and one named Scott'

keys swinging he comes
forward quivering but
true in aim, open
hand to book, jerks back
the jacket strokes
along the spine for flaws,
runs finger down
inner hinge, sniffs flares
at binding,
interrogates the rear
pastedown, rifles
loose sheets, quest abandoned

rubber band peeled from
pale blue Co-Op chequebook

swift signature
knuckle to moist moustache

transaction complete he
shudders to next stand

greener greener pastures

YOU SAW 5 SUNSETS IN 4 DAYS

for B. Catling

breathless on that incline
the best laid

events of the morning of
11.7.85

not to be described
but afterwards in Yeovil

breakfast (£1.06)
sausage bacon tomato egg

& a triangle of bread
crisped in such grease

that the knife as it pressed
squeezed out moist

killing juices
clean white cups

not stalking intent
dragging it on bloody toenails

HURRICANE DRUMMERS SELF-AID
IN HAGGERSTON

'Ronnie Kray is now in Broadmoor and brother Reggie in Parkhurst
from where he is trying... to get a security firm called Budrill off
the ground.'

There's a mob of rumours from s. of the river
challenging teak and shattering glass
with dropkicks honed on GLC grant aid

fake Nike trainers stamp out likely
prints of light, moth-shaped entries.
Another team of semi-skilled dips

work the precinct, dry-cleaning my credits,
licenses and a thin wad of royal portraits:
they collect on unconvincing promises

In reply the locals can offer
a squad car of handy lads looking for lefty,
cruising on fat rubbers that immediately

give the game away, employment prospects
are good for wolf importers, cross-breeders
of beasts with more jaw than brain

The bells! the bells! chime out in celebration,
aerobic heels flash high torque
round the corner of Queensbridge Road

'Hey, what is it about this place?'
say the reverend suddenly
looking out of the window at

a group of black youths as we
approach Dalston
'They're smoking reefer on the street!'

'Music is music,' says Cleveland
'it's the words that separates
gospel from the rest, only the words'

IN THE LATEST PROOF OF ACKROYD

1/4 inch to the W. of
'fibres, hair, ash, burnt paper'
a small insect has died

4 legs attached, the fifth
- and sixth - a mere stain

their substance on the opposite page,
solitary, 1/4 inch to the E. of

'disconcerted Hawksmoor. He
called for a roll of adhesive tape'

TACKY ADMIRALS

1

in Boston (Lincs)
a last cigar

& the wrong place
to smoke it

2

taking G.Swift's *Waterland*
back to the Fens is

like pissing into the Amazon
a relief, but quite pointless

3

in Boston
the nation's reserved books

you can walk, she said
for miles

straight out
into the ocean

KRISTALLNACHT

'When Soutine finally consulted an ear specialist about the terrible earache, in the canal of the painter's ear the doctor discovered, not an abscess but a nest of bedbugs.'

escape with the children but
escape them we cannot, will not
draw up beyond this breath:
beeswax burning in an old tin cup

break the ring with
a child's soft head before
it's too late, it is
already, cold fear

glove turned, waxy smoke
boiled honey evoking
a woman's blood-string
does not arouse

it terrifies & the protection
which is this room marked
with square posts
becomes a place of torment

the children we
discover in ourselves are
drained, stars
on the curve of their lids

night without beginning
runs wild as a scalded dog

SIGNIFICANT WRECKAGE
(1988)

SIGNIFICANT WRECKAGE

'The isle is full of noises'

The Turk sent his catamite swimming to shore
in quest of one perfect juice-tight grape:
salt-stiff lips, skin torn on thorn,
sandstone profiles in the cliff, returned
risk suppressed in this violation, branch broken
    burnt alive, barbecued
    on the hillside, smoke visible
    a mile out, across tame, shaming water

When the statues walked, I slept
and could not move, so set
that muscles confined in plaster seemed
wet: low sleep presses an imprint of
breath's fern into a chalkwhite ceiling

Moulded angels cradle the instruments
that cut them free from an account of life:
skinner's blade, sharktooth saw, adze
    paleness is excused, boiled
    in olive oil, rashered peeled or
    dropped in pits

Each village celebrates its translation;
a mute in the tower slams the clapper
rocking the skirted bell in which he squats
...flies are the knots that have escaped

A wall of disease mementoes - rags
bandages, crutches & coloured photographs -
swallows all taint of fever, they age
in a dream of dim sepsis and privileged pain

2

Accusing fingers, supplicating bones
are snapped, dropped from the path,
evolve to lizard or to gecko-life,
escape the station, abrupt as fretted cocks

Words wriggle in a heat that
slides them from the icing page.
The saint becomes a lectern
to the truth: unburied, newborn
nakedness, fish-naked, not unclothed

Break them with hammers and they yield
no sound, heartless, untongued.
Villagers recage their passions,
and the flaws: no need
to stave pirates or to choke the well

Stoic, they watch
death tighten the web, grow
skin for aboriginal flight: a chill
ledge for griddled sun, & spite

3

Swimming the salt & sticky with pearls,
glove-fish, you are trapped in an abstract
of grace. Float the world, glazed to curve,
sky-free, cloudless: rock, cave & alder copse

It sits as legend, is recalled:
the candle flame, detached from lard,
under hot ground, black mushroom cap
of our guide, his damaged recitative

The primal version is untold, but
flares in flash-lit eyes, a panic red!

Figs burst between your fingers.
The island is barren in its dust and flags.
They lift blind saints onto pedestals with
swaying cranes, deafen them with thunderflashes

Brotherhood of marching bands & shirts
that are too tight, secret signs. The police
in scorched glasses, guns. Barebreasted,
a German woman under the Christ stack.
Crones mutter, pull knuckle. Lovers wrestle
in mannerless surf, disgendered, scapegoat

4

Travesties of dwarf strength, they scale
cane ladders with cheesestone blocks,
cutting into their shoulders. The White Goddess
in death-drag, red-mouthed, spitting out
pomegranate seeds, split figs, semen, hair

An island-skull lit by blades, rubric
of goat and incense, faked bells,
confessions broadcast to the wind

A heresy of beards restages cultic
feasts; migrant birds are
netted, overcooked. The wine
is scented, peeling teeth. Principality
of hills, dogs, stars...

A place to quit. The circuit of the sea
erases pique: juniper logs and cedar

In catalogue-fresh ruins, the amphitheatre
of some discharged Herod, we sit
beneath a rage of crucified leper waxworks,
backs turned from a dark
feathering of smoke, blown seawards

The splash, white ankles offered to the rope

San Lawrenz, Gozo

JACK ELAM'S OTHER EYE
(1991)

'wie anders sei noch geschlafen als stehend'

Paul Celan (trans. Michael Hamburger)

'how else shall anyone sleep but standing'

JACK ELAM'S OTHER EYE

*'The black psychosis which many psychoanalysts now
assume lies at the base of consciousness'*

letter never sent, of things you didn't see
the pheasant outside my leaking keyhole
bright beak & wobbly neck, always stiff tail
associated with the verb KILL and next
the sharpened fin of rock they call
BLACK, from which it is not so easy
to spot the secret ruins of the abbey,
trout pond or damp trees...

even sympathetic natives give these a miss

single-bar electric fire, embroidered cushion
black & white tv, not
fearing the dust-mouthed presence that
is forever here; more, much more
than my telling of it, speaking aloud
is all I have to say: a bell

enclosed in a slatted turret, a hump of grass
less real than the pictures on the wall

only *then* will we know what confinement means

Clay Cottage, Hay on Wye

THERMOMETERS OF THE DAMNED

running into wind that tunnels a fist
through burning orange stacks
a hard circuit, so he spits his own self-
poison as a cooling dart of
slobber back across the cheek to
nestle, hanging in scarlet jogger's caul

the smoking heap is safely caged on
old football grit now grown over:
doors open, a thin fine light
to palliate deconstruction of library fear

the King of Angels is another kind of hood
& needs a new scribe, wings for
bow, helmet-pain, splinters of blood,
smoke is female

and what he breathes he also loves

CRAZY AS IN RAZOR

'I adhere to the Ten Commandments except when it's bad for business'
James Ellroy

the audience is a Jew & the Audience is not
he wants something he is quite indifferent to
he wants something but not badly he wants it
fluently around him gilded air so he sits
guarded & calm behind sweating belly
hanging over tourniquet of silken cummerbund

he wants ceremony not the slash of poetry
he wants to own it he wants the gush of
oyster holes in satin *he wants it all*
the flipside of a fur mat no detail no
abstraction nor any kind of map thread
followed to an unexploitable conclusion

flawed ourselves, grim goys, we curse &
do without earning praise no
casket no visiting raptors of guilt

the river dies of inattention slowly when
he quits the salon to smoke a thick wrist

SCARPS & GREEN HEAPS

opposite the scrapyard & across the river
we were walking apart but calmly
in the same direction linked the noisy
anger of a spurned machine a moveable grab
producing nothing more than the satisfied crunch
of digested automobiles & erased traffic

the threat disturbed your
sense of occasion hardly at all

a few yards of clear sand finite shelf
of pebbled egg fragments of green-glass
well worth picking over & thus beyond our means

losing sight of the river itself
to stoke our appetites on a crust
of pink fishmeat blue-oil smoke
persuaded from a lettuce leaf

no call to go further & we came back
well over the limit a sidelong glance
at the morbid stalk of Canary Wharf

then at it like a whole tray of bright cutlery
exploiting opportunity metal buffers clanging
appreciation of the hurricane's diminishing tail

want it enough & you can, have it all

RECOVERY & DEATH

late daisies, burnt leaves
curl at the edge
in currents of moist air

silver sun stirs a high tumbler
dark pool among tree-tops

LEON IS A TRAMP.
And his mother is a slag.
And she wears shit shoes
That cost £1.99p

bench not designed for rest
resolutely, his back
to the scene he is describing

POGROM MUSIC

'Armageddon with mirrors.'

aniline dye travels faster than my will permits
slides dutiful penetrates targeted source of
unlicensed growth, proud to glow in
negative plates orthodox heresies opulent tissue
must yield to the district's blade: cut clean, burnt

& the sun proceeds unmoved among cirric threads
passing through fixed points on the thong
that held Apollinaire's shattered skull in place
not quite in time closing on
the immaculate balance of Christ Church tower

at length warm a private place easy
among roofs slates slatboard shifts
they frame a patch of sunlight & innocently
fan motes empty as the *Angelus* stain
now shocked blitz wallpaper hears
a wooden pace rabbi & his daughter dividing
the ceiling over balconies of memorial art

defend yourself in childbirth or split
a scarlet pomegranate: 'your voice...our deacon'
sudden mosses cold pools revealed among boards
a potential man making his curse
forbidding a future
that has prematurely surveyed our corkscrew bones

logging the debris of unrecorded necks & ties
a room suffers more to be returned
than ever it can grant in recompense
nothing to falsify the register of ruin whose cities
are already known & damned in carbon air

all we transcribe is mute affection

SOLITARY AFFRAYS

the old woman who talks to birds
is a man also the space in which he
conducts himself is sealed with cages
he is caged can blindly turn
face to the world over
in the calm before a midnight raid
opaque barrier innocent
of sledges & sharp crystals underfoot

whoever designed those Holly Street
flats, corridors one hundred yards &
lurker lifts, phantom dogs, would
in a saner society be properly rewarded
by a blindfolded firing squad

a few minutes is more than
he can bear retreats orange door
at street level locked &
real woman slippered mouth agape
greenwinter coat plods slowly away

successful only / in escaping from my sight

MALDOR FURS

midnight daughters splice the lemon summons
herded together in saltbaths eager to answer

who calls & who remembers

let the empty picture-book flick
on a scrubbed oak table: steppe wind

seems the only *rational* explanation & sure
the least worthy to nominate

a devil's teat / growing from my finger

NIL BY MOUTH

among the unfumigated lungs of the poor
naked ears parboiled
brazen hoops piercing thin cartilage
they plod towards allowance pension virgin cash
BANG goes the punch promises promises
shuffle in on themselves screened always
NEXT elbows forward in case
it should all turn out to be exactly what it is
just another paper fraud

are Lee Harwood's clients anything like this?

wanting a mere stamp to ship a book
seems decadent & extreme
lives of the not quite desperate ourselves
coughing dust of official sanction
too far gone to appreciate
the counter clerk's degraded shirt
John Cage doodles scoring the chorus
gobbing sputum expulsion
the dim the dull mirror-reversed scene

necks of knotted flesh horsetail hair
tied with silly rags the only place
where there is world enough to write

CHERNOBYL PRIESTS

there is death in us we are all sick &
the electric typewriter rattles its dying spasm
life unzipped slowly from a gashed throat
fishbone cuts flesh: phantom hedge-strimmer

fallen out of gravity of love to travel
solitary in a straight line tracked
by what we are tracking the silverback
train of fate scalded express
that does not appear to suffer or to move

children raising khaki sheets to their lips
old women at prayer perched along the sill
heated until they crack the varnish splits

in prolonged silence pastry sinks
a pie of bandages or sheep escape the pot
spilling earth & pellets of hot grey dung

aslant parquet impact of desert-sand
nobody dares protest infirm terrain
sunbathers nude among smoking ruins
where official portraits used to hang & who
will nominate which photographs to burn

BREATHING IS THE SAME METHOD AS DROWNING

razor sex white as memory debate
volunteers graciously through
abandoned greed: greed going critical

joy & spit lubricate a deep well
'go down,' I said, 'go down'
offering modern bucket & thin rope

tools encountered years later
in a Belfast police station

see them shuffle provincial trains hot
on the trail of an unbreakable engagement
flighted plasma rushed to understand
the locking system the timing chain

a black stain lifts like radio noise
air raid repudiated as most news is
all untrustworthy especially pictures
of which there can never be enough

prophetically the land blanks & rushes
to jeer at our stationary carriage

GIN HAD NO CONNECTION WITH TIME

for Douglas Oliver

out of the cloister the poetry reading fugitive faces
'wind down your window please sir'
the parked car, Patrick notes, files our registration
he also had something to say about those pillars
petering out in unashamed abdication of meaning
a folded heap of well-ironed convict shirts

it is always the one with the rimless spectacles
who gets to speak: *Girton or the Crematorium*
we'll never it's true in this life achieve
Ian Patterson's house not on this weary circuit

we pound the Bateman & Panton streets our heads
bereft of numbers & even try one door, 45, to honest
incredulity: *the poet preaches as a silk of silver*
threads a discourse, cape reversed, his audience
cavort in joy to hear confirmed what they already know

& coughing the outside essayist quits the salon
to eavesdrop, in quotation, from a distant door

we are all here make of our congregation
what you will the greyhead the woman
in a boy's pink sweater the lovers of truth

but this stuff has become so *peculiar*
there's no audience for it no close reader
imagine that, good, the reader who will never
thank god step forward to declare herself

it hurts only women know
there is still some centre that might work
& do not refuse to shout for it or sing

THE CARNAL GATE: HITMAN IN PRIVATE GARDEN
(*LAMB HOUSE, RYE*)

as the circuit of the garden is an oval sentence
its staging posts pets' graveyard draw breath
sit on the wet slats of a white bench
celebrating a spring shower or gardener's hose
when this climax of meaning tips the alcove news of
Charlie 'The Silent Man' Wilson cooking the trumpet
spitting scarlet rumours across poplin sheets how
a 'pale youth' rang the anniversary bell to gain access
walked him out towards the lapping pool intent
on a bit of business but landing first a sneaky blow
side of the nose kneed him with enough force
to show up on the pathologist's report eased
the oiled barrel intimately against or into his mouth
& blew away the roof of his skull

Henry James's holograph tended to droop
towards the margin black ink revisions
the famous library regathered I can't recall
a kinder evening setting sun over red roofs
English ladies counting coin fearing deficit
I strolled without knowledge Charlie
would be cremated along with a dog won
in a poker game their sympathetic ashes mingled

when my father's blue pen died I changed hands
reaching into the drawer for the slim silver affair
my wife gave me once again picking up the original
a posthumous spurt enough as if the nib had
simply *debated* its passage across
resistant grease of the notebook's pre-lined page

a mortal strain trembling through my arm

THE SHAMAN'S POUCH (*MANISH, ISLE OF HARRIS*)

unyielding, the pliancy of
night's sprung ribs

from which we build
a darkness

in which nothing lives
& life is felt & fur & brine

2

writing distances
the cumulative world

barter of detail
hail of sound

impulse to clarify
through obscurity

to say it over &
mar by definition

stone-eyes tick
the question is avoided

BOAT DRESSES

for Steve & Joan Dilworth

whisky & flakes of green leaf,
fish-oil, pink stone meat
spilling its lucid fat

a lung-feather in throat
breaks crow tarpaulin,
the sorrow of a buried wing

death is an easier thing,
blackwater nights press
sweat from the moor's bones

leave now, left ticking
out, beyond graveyard sand
the chest of swords

a dying tree
an empty church
a spear-cage

vertical narrative / of unchanging names

CAMERA OBSCURA (*OXFORD*)

Lepidopterist of memory. Of ice-erasure. The road.
Bone chants. Moustaches wet with yak butter. Glacial
debris in slack mouth: a lost tooth sibilates

Pink blood on the outhouse wall, he
passes childhood, dreads to hear truth's lure.
Or: wire slices harelip with heavy-duty blade

We live in sound retrace the rasp of curses,
carbon-breath lifting paper from dying eye. Love
in a jar. Things happen often & again

As milk to mercy runs the disks you name
are anklebones, pendulum of hazard. Scarlet insects
shriek in a clock. Sheathed fingers tap final storm

Now lightning reverie speaks, approaching core.
Bruises on the tongue spit venom, lily pads.
A whiskey bottle seen as swallowed telescope

Father's throat open to surgical intervention.
Essence of brass. Goldwatch gobbed against abused
lid of Hasidic trilby in a cobbled London lane

Tabled on microphone-altar, the painted revelation
broadcasts a city's silence. Taboo of candlefat, dew
of sexual transmission. Hard bench of paradox

THE DOUBLE'S DOUBLE

(UNCOLLECTED)

THE DOUBLE'S DOUBLE

There were no mirrors in the attic, the investigator said. And not much light. A single, thin beam through a knot in the wood. Floorboards had been nailed over the absence of a window. What he noticed, principally, was the sound of running water.

Gush gush gush. And nothing to be found. Dry as dust. Dust everywhere: little conical heaps - as if rats had devoured the old man's library and shat out clinker.

–How old was he when he disappeared?

No response.

–You must have some idea. Twenty? Sixty?

–There were children's toys in a drawer with a collection of false teeth. Inscribed photographs of music hall stars and detective books that hadn't even been published when it happened...

–What? What happened?

–The incident. The vanishing.

–What were the titles of the books?

–You'll be shocked. There was a Jeffrey Archer. I picked it up, handled it. *As the Crow Flies*. In Japanese. Or Chinese. Title printed in English. Red bus on the cover. A number 14, Putney Heath. Outside Harrods. The royal crest. Archer's book starts around here, Whitechapel. It's a Whitechapel story. The old man kept a diary. There were a number of alphabet letters, torn out of some magazine, stuck to the wall. The rabbi's son-in-law reckoned he was teaching himself to read.

This was the story of the scholar, the hermit in the attic. Dust golem. He had come into being to oppose the glittering advance of the city, the surveillance screen, the self-reflecting towers. He was imagined because he was necessary. And then he was forgotten.

–Who tells the story?

–An actor, a writer. It doesn't matter.

–How does it end?

He laughed.

The letters on the wall made things happen. They shifted. Everything shifted. Nail the door shut on the mystery, let it fester. Seal it with seven seals. Come back in twenty years. Now there are more books, more pans. A junkshop joanna, an old upright with half the keys flat as Sunday morning's paypacket. It wasn't there before, not in any of the photographs. And he'd stuck letters to the keys, somebody had. Alphabet letters. Making up words, combinations. Making things happen. You'd be taking a real chance to play that thing. Ghost music.

He didn't need mirrors, that's my theory. There were two of him. Breathe on a bowl of shaving water and he'd turn it to slate. It's the only plausible explanation. He's there and he's not there. The sound of a river rushing beneath the floorboards, washing away dust. And him on his knees, eye to a crack, looking for his reflection. That room is his confession. You can play it like a crystal set. You can stand there and listen to the voices of angels who have fallen through time.

RAISING THE GOLEM

It was the doctor, one of them, one of those Jacks they talk so much about. Face like a falcon. Wide-brimmed beaver to hide what was passing between left eye and right. A quack. A tent-show medicine man. Glasgow Irish. Anti-Semite. They say he could raise the dead, Gladstone bag filled to the brim with salty foreskins. Some reckon he was a foreigner, Yid, low German. Some take the other tack, swear that he picked his teeth with nails pulled from the true cross. He always lived here. Ask any of the old ones to show you his gravestone in the burial ground behind the charity flats. Scrape lichen from deep-cut lettering. DOCTOR SYENITE, it spells. The Paddies call him the Cunning Man. The Hasids call him Reuben. Poles pay him in feathers and claws.

He was the one who made a man. Not, as you would, any proper person, with a bride from the backroom of the Seven Stars: but like Frankenstein before him, or the Rabbi of Prague. He made a city-man, shaped him from clay.

By the collaboration of the four - *Aysch, Mayim, Ruach, Aphar* - was made the Golem of the fourth element. Not river mud, sour poultice. Finest red clay from the brickfields. Complete in all his members, the size of him had young girls blushing, running off, coming back for another peep. He was tamed to the doctor's purpose, laid out in the field of Matfelon, where they say a church had once been.

This golem was in Cable Street, taking on six blackshirts at a time. He swallowed cobblestones and spat them straight back at the horses. He was mucker with Jack Spot. Before he was Jack. Went down with him in the motor to Brighton. He stood against the Saffron Hill Mob when they came at him twelve-handed. He made politicians drink their rivers of blood. And made sure he pissed in there first.

What happened? The creature got old like the rest of us. Started to take himself seriously. To believe what chancers wrote about him. He traced his legend into comic books with a finger the size of a saveloy. Pictures anyway.

The pride of him. As if his attic were the entire world, the sun and the moon and the planets. When the city sold its soul, he went with it.

What became of the Doctor, you say? Who do you think is doing the buying? Who got the Brewery and the Market? Who is telling you this story?

WHAT THE HERMIT WROTE IN HIS DIARY

I
I AM
I AM FOR
I FASTEN
I GARNISH
I HAVE BEEN
I HAVE BEEN PLACED
I HAVE SETTLED
I HAVE TALKED
I MADE LAW
I MADE MAN
I MADE YOU
I MOVE YOU
I MOVE

UNDER
UNDER WHOM
UNDER WHOSE
UNDER WHOSE WINGS
UNDERSTAND
UNDER FIRE
UNDER YOU

UNDEFILED

HOW THE MESSAGE WAS BROUGHT

Doctor Syenite had a book in which the names of the living had been printed. Those, in that part of the city, outside the walls, who would live through the coming year. One corner of the penultimate page had been torn, defaced. The hermit's name was missing. Nobody knew his name. He had no birth certificate. His mother was buried and his sister taken away. That was the reason he wasn't there. Doc Syenite had nothing to concern himself with. Unnamed was unbegotten.

The doctor went from door to door checking the others. Coins were dropped into the depths of his hat. Lowlifers called him ganef, a racketeer. But what was this pathetic tithe against the guarantee he offered? Another year of life. 'My word,' he would say. 'You got my word on it.' A priest. And he behaved like a tallyman.

His long coat clinked as he walked. He'd forgotten one man. The hermit with the letters pasted to the wall. The unholy fool had torn a corner from the page. He studied the mystical properties of colour. Letters for words. But he didn't know how colour tasted. What sounds the different colours made. Syenite was blue. Blue was the word the hermit was meditating on.

The doctor smiled, he saw the humour of it, when his shadow moved away from its host. Back into carbonised dirt on Portland stone. Back through the dark porch of the church. Away from him. His shoulders felt like someone had torn off a yard of sticking plaster, body hair, warts and all. It stung and he liked it. Wings clipped with nail scissors.

PENGUIN MODERN POETS 10
(1996)

FRIENDLY FIRE

better wander the town
than rest your cheek
on some desk's astonished surface

hair-cracks, skull cracks, acid stains
of book-cleaning operations
risk flight: the sweating cloth & map

screwed into armpit like
a rivet, a conquered bubo

it's only by report that I
screamed in the night
a bent horizon
twitching of black
upper branches, soot hangovers

mad as crow, axle-slicked
bloody gobbets in teeth &
dog excrement coating dry lips

new nights, light beyond interpretation
railway barracks hissing platforms
ice trains stalled for want of paper

not even, not ever, not now
writing ourselves out of the story

IMMACULATE CORRUPTIONS

i.m. Angela Carter

'boiled cabbage & gin hanging in the air'
bird-skid, delayed nostalgia of heavy plant
essays a tight arterial road, Cambridge
and The North...

tart's black stockings, kites upstairs
mature fright-wig doubling for
the infant mistress scurrying home

I refuse
play of reflections
in portrait glass, light from outside
all the dark truths
that shade your profile in the reeve
of our child's bedazzled sunburst head

bright slate roof...

indifferently, the vanished cat
late wasps & broken coffee bowl

will endure always & live & shine

SANCTUARY KNOCKER

*'The only respect in which he was a Christian was the interest
he shared with Christ in professional women.'*
                                                Edward Dorn

the telephone rests on Swedenborg Yeats too &
WH Hodgson, *The Master Map of London*
lunch booked in revamped chophouse better days
known less on table costing more, borderline
dyke she says she's been sick for months City
within a city the holy well, yes, we're all dead soon
has any single human survived
they've jawed about it certainly brushed chalk
from shoulder hair the former
novelist wants to try ladies' clothes wants
rephrase that to talk about drink
time curdling like a refulgent turd Bruce
Chatwin forgot to shoot desert road uncensored
censoring a sharp pain in the neck inherited
from a Mortlake gravestone not one sentient being
on this planet knows who Helen Redpath was

A GROUP OF MEN, ALL CALLED JOHN

mid-afternoon / lazy bars
across undipped headlamps

a scarlet Jag 4.2
against a green pub

& William Carlos Williams
is still dead

PRECIOUS & STRAW

whistle of the cat-catcher in the night
native Londoner with his wriggling sack

plunder hair & fogged skin
pouching grey laurel lint

keeping craft tradition
- severed hand - alive

20,000 books feed on the barber's lungs
a granite stall aborts his son's display

coal beach /
half-hunters shovelled on felt

damp mortar, creamstone hedge
& lost documentation expelling verse

WHERE THE TALENT IS

i.m. Derek Raymond

sweating bread & Colombian coffee
fires the missing date
a cheap watch clicks lunchhour
pushing scribe towards
a hard-earned amnesiac seizure

hot as the thought of hell:
keys, fever beads

we send for Polaroids to confirm our loss

the symbol in the cemetery avenue
overreaches itself lacks sap in the vein
Herne-horns of living ash

better far to visit
than to have this place described

THAT WHICH APPEARS

as old men dancing return sap to springboard
not needing nor wanting, not needing
bank's yellow blood, earth scalded in urine

so far beyond the rule of zero
(footpath closed by criminals with faded ribbons)
we set a water-compass at true north & zip it
serene inside the flap of sheepskin before
renting a surrogate to forget the whole matter

'off to the Orkneys in small stages'
read the suicide note of Cynthia Nolan

MORE KISSING THAN TEACHING

cinema flag (on clean white pole)
a fast American breakfast
'The Gateway to the Cotswolds'

REVENGE OF THE RIVER HORSE

celebrate the loss of rain
losing outside sounds that fret on glass
thin as membrane dividing that which is
not to be known / from all the rest

sliding slipping following
the stream down the mountain
vertical excited strokes: a pigeon-hook
shaped in steel to caress
the coldness of your back the cancer-
granting, cancing-saving fern
View from the Gantry
slate bright as moonlight on coal
wise children conceived in porcelain tubs

the spokes of an upturned bicycle
hum at the bedside
in a reviving, prophylactic hymn

no saddle no reprieve
black fly-breath of a snipered mule

TRAVELLERS BY APPOINTMENT ONLY

leaves heavy as shed skin
and suicide is the hook in the throat

a mad person unsexed in her shout

unwilling to vanish she sticks
like the stink of your best friend's shit
sprayed from aerosol to offend
a cornershop that defies geometry by
standing at the centre of a bent triangle

swiftly the Asian shirt rushes forward
not refusing cigarette custom
greeting instead with fumigation

fuck, fuck words we can't quite
hear, china gums bared, black cavity
she plunges headlong skating
on cones of steaming dogshit

single slipper
privates sluiced at a public tap

READ MY LISP

let crows with their cutpurse habits
                have it
oily meadows & all meat
the city spits out
                let them kaw
mobhanded, gorblimey & selfish as
old hoods, memory thieves in apple-
green rooms waiting on bad news

let crows expose naked trees
fat as gristle kebabs
louder than something you
petrol-burn alive

'let him have it chris'

colourless air / blue bomber-cap
on balcony the ape-fit
pensioner who used to lift shirts
a solitary professional
abusing shelves tastes ink of
tabloid rage uncivil tongue

it's our town the crows know
chalk worms in starry ground
a hung carpet of clystered smoak

BLIND MENDOZA'S TALLOW SAUCER

In oyster bars / shells
fill with borrowed hair, so track
the taste an unsuspected trip -
lefthand spiral to flatter dome
lick out lardmeat & avoid
the drop: satin thong silk mosaic
home for TV, clergy. Orange 2-bar
fizzing like irradiated corncob
wedged in cheek, *yes sah boss.*
Morningside grin & coiffured flick
costs more than decommissioning
a presidential Boeing. Random bombers
pick up hefty credits spreading oil &
flesh across battery-lit purple snow

vibrating finger deletes dusty screen

INSOMNIA

a man can fall backwards from a window
& live or die according to the requirements of the script
& it can happen in the Renoir Bloomsbury
or the Arts Cinema Cambridge
the coat in question, black slicker, vanishes forever
'you're wearing my stuff' she says

unable to sleep I read William Burroughs
his book of dreams (a lie)
unable to sleep I write unable to sleep
I read William Burroughs his book of dreams
(not true) thinking of Catherine Blake who
sat for hours beside her husband
whose 'inspirations' threatened to 'tear him asunder'
graved (local) voices of retrospective prophecy

recovered from suburban flicks, we applaud
'a young PT instructor shooting cats with an air-rifle'
the missing hyphen of *Stumbling Block*
the proof of that curious name, Kells Elvins
the dry boast: 'bring me a leper & I will kiss it'

THE EBBING OF THE KRAFT

'The only English word I knew was "yes".'
                                    Willem de Kooning

Like a butcher I relish the drive to work
poplars primed with glycerine
who wants to observe the stealth of nature
cathedral icehouse where all hats are white &
regimental crombies crack like sodden wood
drying out in a tax inspector's office.
The kill is stockings & meat. Hanged buds
in wild orchards where children
scrump for soap.
Taps run blood to wash away water
our road is clean as bridal linen. In the old house
with its marsh-gas boiler a wife
distempers what I leave behind, strapped
gloves on which the wool still grows
blackberries to spit on pristine sheets

as wait we must for the summoned stranger
the mannerless oak

'the dove which is brought back to life by the hawk'

DIRTY DANCING AT THE ROEBUCK

So much can be said when walls are left
standing by themselves revealed at last
the secret no longer worth the keeping, old
man enlightened suspicious of his son holding
down the mortem of history: dust
instead of air. Cancel the stench of leashed
dog its brute circumference, apron & spike
No ice in the bucket no purple heel to sip
The site is a film of powdered stone
brought to ground
a gesture of unmindful erasure.
Bones dance against that wall
crime is longer than life
shadows driven underground
a river of lost voices
The beast in the thicket curious
about split prism the starburst news-
flash of the hunter's sporting rifle

PARADISE ROW

hang-loose journos decant stateside w/cash
pillows that painters could usefully burn

an advertised woman's hairshirt extension
topiarizes muff to fluffy wembley heart

the deal lacks food the lapdancer
takes too much on herself she won't
read the plaintiff his regal quiff

auteur étrangers & folk who live in exile
without knowing it feel at home
wherever they trull from a foreign bed

Menilmontant lifts from cemetery wall
cash that cheque, sir, before it unrolls

a carpet underlay & the white phone
shrills to query in camera evidence

GLIBBERY ELECTRICAL

'Looking back, my throat has always been my Achilles heel.'
Jacqueline Bisset

iceblue shoulderbands against wetpink door
the immutable flat cap & hands in leisure wear
each day, key in fist, nowhere special to go
shop sold shop closed Parkinson's Disease
& Parkinson (Hoxton Square) doesn't want it
back home with soggy roll of recent newsprint
confirming the worst, implants blessed by Rome
qualities beyond description: balcony life
to shelf life, too far from the deck old creeper

$1^1/_2$ tablets of something like Prozac
as *digestif* of choice after 3 or more solid pints
greenish-white the boy
buggered on WC's checkerboard floor, not worth
the call out a dull & dusty wind
ambulances lose their way across the marshes

he returns opens his hutch enters leaves
again almost immediately the elaborate
pantomime of the lock-up, spying out the ledge
strangling his string-dog with public affection

hot food brings news of fear in foil trays
airline scoff for those who do not travel
dramatic fissure of the medial ligament
everything above the palate dies in sympathy

SUB (NOT USED): MOUNTAIN

prize cicatrix in oil suspension
charts flap proud from damp walls
which are themselves charts
of islands where swamps are undeclared
the superseded house
brutish topiary of an illegitimate bride
weather systems register a pigeon shed
my lord at his grouse table
filing his second rank of teeth
will you risk the caretaker's gamey taupe
black worm lives reluctant in altar bread
no hermaphrodite pope whose lard finger
slips a fat ring over chicken bone

strapped into rented ligatures
he stomps the town
dragging Kent
& all her oasts behind him

EGG ROLLING IN A STONE AGE CULTURE

atrophy of idiolect
atrophy of pearls & peaches
steam on lip of brandy balloon
absinthe from a sherry schooner
coral island in Medway's qwag
peppermints dispensed by gloved hands
snuff on a spinnaker
unhurried asbestos to lace the lungs

many golden cuirasses of oilseed rape
& two women with the initials *JC*

pylon wires trench the land
kneejerk colours in the classroom
boat-hats & starfish pasties
drink up you lads at the sunset bar
punish mulattos & mestizas whose
children fly the coop unable to face
the rented grandiloquence of brazen crofts

BUNHILL FIELDS

'Secretly, he loved poetry.'
                Tim Hilton (on Clement Greenberg)

the proximate fig shades a shale envelope
writing I have no intention of writing this
heavy leaves green fed with grey fed up caught
between showers noted shadows where
William & Catherine lie loose disinterred
a glazed brown pot in clay dead flowerheads
flower-smelling water incoherent autumn
sunlight free-associating through stone flags when
the blonde child on her precious red bicycle
what did you say these were called again what did
you say *figs* yes figs figs but do they have seeds
confirmation speeds her uncertain way
balanced five-in-hand that might have ripened
juice of the vertical slab unsteady from wine lunch
a mossy cushion obelisks & peeled plaster faces
scarlet seeds on a thick black tongue

THE EXHIBITION I DIDN'T HOLD AT THE TATE WOULD HAVE INCLUDED

(1) $^1/_2$ the pickled brain of Wyndham Lewis

(2) the mantle of Powhatan

(3) the Tradescants' missing Ark

(4) the peeled skin of Lord Archer's back
     (with its psychogeographic moles)

(5) a silent video of J.H. Prynne's famous lecture on
     Willem de Kooning's *Rosy-Fingered Dawn at Louse Point*

(6) Jeremy Bentham mummified in a perspex Panopticon

(7) The River Thames

OTHERING THE ANGELS

for David & Judy Gascoyne

comestible sunlight refined by the cherry tree's pink
machinery, October on the island
a lucky limbo & unearned audience with a perky revenant,
Chris Petit's Sharp freezing this moment's fan
to disclose the Terror of Europe, chocolate stealth, leafjig
or, anecdotes of Dr Bluth Conrad Veidt Anna Kavan
an armful of ox-blood & methedrine before the royal blue taxi
skids to a halt at the palace gates:
'do you realise this land is reborn? Jerusalem & all her angels?'

marmoreal segments of fruitcake splinter a floral plate
resinous waves over the dancing table, murmurs
of parchment & ancient photographs packed like Egyptian
leaves under sticky laminate: Chairman Ginsberg in New York,
Robert Duncan wall-eyed in San Francisco, future memories
hoarded, journals recovered, get it over before it happens again

the director's caramel Merc & plainsman shirt £300 reduced
leather jacket from Harrods justifies a silent movie
'nearly as good, almost the same' the poet says, reliving
conversations from an abandoned book, sliding upstairs
to his throne in the tick of an insulated book-lined room

ivy on the rim. 'welcome' on blackboard at the door
french lessons in the window convex mirror
sunset over a milk shore. prisoners issued with acrylic
pencils. the daily poem. 'residual hope'

THE EBBING OF THE KRAFT
(1997)

One has
the other
where
treads
of death
closely

TOURISM

DEGAUSSING THE WOLFMAN

for Francis Stuart

is the yellow twin on a straight country road
a thrash of wild palms in warm august rain
a split car, discrete, neither 'blue' nor 'white'

this fine old man laughs at previous convictions
his teeth the foil tines of a garden fork
no time to spare
stalled landscape alert to the pleasure of drowning
laminate booklets identify birds, unobtainable wines
he's paid his dues old devil been numbered
in track & cloud, dust-cellars of ruined cities
now presses inky thumb to the custard of
cricket whites: lift the blue-lead page & what
you'll see is a droplet of menstrual blood

'drift all drift' says the knob-nosed Irishman

MULLET GARDENS

Shadows of hammer-headed daffodils yolk mismatched stripes of human sawdust. The unsuspected charm of morning tables. A bitter yellow taste distinguishes the chill of beaker water. (David Jones in Shoreham: shallow views in a tall window.) *You're never going to feel any friskier.* This is it, salty residues simmering in a black pan. Crystals clog butter, ceramic shields of dyed cornlets. Each meal recalling the last until your flesh-lip mushrooms & a thatch of green fouls the Cubist jug. So press his head in a vice to make the eyeballs large enough to see coats that bring gold away from shocked skin. Ear trumpets: each caller more choked with phlegm. Each message less worthy of the messenger.

OCEAN ESTATE

fording pondlife to pamper your Arab steed
rosettes displayed above pillows
of cleanest straw, can't call
a whippet a dog (it's a bitch anyway &
hot to smear my shiny strides)

call it: 'long-term rewards of academic life'

all the blood-fruit wine that
flatters & does not grind the loaf you
squeeze cutting an X-ray pet
who has mislaid her silver bell

'forest' no threat so much green
stacked until you close out
the other stuff the bearded litigants
incubating harm (despoiling
place) too pedigree'd to fart in tune

poets outgun symposium novelists
having less to say & saying it
with more conviction & smelling
like they live by choice in mismatched
suits (obligated to Burton's black)

a fust of old books & older cheese
nobody loves gossip like these salaried dudes

above us hangs a carmine cloud
the amputated leg of Harry Crews
stern invoice of what a writer's biography
should entail: no kids & a drawful of
biro caps to clean wax from the ears

granted, all dream
but some of us, having better manners,
would never admit so much

HALF OF PLUS *(DURHAM)*

under the castle's ox / red stone
I baste oxters I bathe
green foam, gorgeous: too many
southrons on the square,
cricket's slack & the river curdles
to pig iron, how many drafts

how many angels
balance on a whalebone pin?

40 miles as the crow files
 - which crow? - to Lindisfarne
that visionary instant, breath
in mouth, never never
to be repeated, no crows oblige

read the culture thus: Bernard
('I'm in the book') MacLaverty gives tongue
in the M & S duplicate of
my favourite blackcurrant shirt
confess: I hoard a biography of Lord Archer
to unravel the long ride home

LANDSCHAFT *(OXFORD)*

no camera gun so the rain slides unthinking
rapturous from glass & by arrangement
into a stone basin where it can recover its poise
lie still the light is green as polyester cooler
than you'd expect of a sanctioned hothouse

imagined snakes press against the cloth of your
loden coat facing behind the century plant warm
earth breathes faster than an hour in the gym
flowers & fades while need sustains bands
of perfume charge us where we lack for sound

raised dome becoming a machine should
cast its portent, baguettes denied, postscript
to hermit art primitive reds & greens torture
of delight naked bodies writhing on the spike
the Jews Mound map deeded not to touch

all we own 31,936 km walk around the world
true Spandau ballet danced in a cell TV weather
voyage taped in a Beirut cellar the last 12 years
are the worst word-blisters held too long in
the mouth Listerine no substitute for speed

shirt off the rest to follow coming close to admitting
an automobile surprised by mirror of other street
poets paired calm & restless bladder stretched
her teeth the precise route to annul the mind
shapes rock-sand to a 4-post yell – *oh yes!* – (& how)

DELETED, NOT DESTROYED

i.m. Eric Mottram

The performance artist is criminal, one of the privileged of the city. He is made tame, this Bedlamite, to pose white against a darkened stairwell. He endures the trance of travel, madness feigned to implicate a procession of disengaged witnesses. Once it took a bribe to poke stick into straw, rattle chains. Now testosterone sponsorship gifts transatlantic flight. Ruffians with razor'd skulls are a transported underclass, flashing burgundy passport tattoos. They colonize deserts that scorpions have abandoned. They feed on ash from a dustbin lid. Swill pus. In the grip of an induced nightmare, they map a journey: 'one inch to the hour.' Durational exercises have been devised to heal the mind of its trash. The gaunt medium, brain burnt to gruel, is fraudulent, but the wound he unzips is an authentic door. Sometimes he pounces on the wrong woman, the one who is not a plant. Sometimes he is attacked.

Only then can the bride ascend to service her bachelors (why must she wear black?). That thing in her mouth is a pen, a torch. Film stock curls a pubic beard. She sings of exile to keep self from screaming an accusation: 'Rapist! Despoiler! Devourer of unborn children!' Shrill sound, bounced from dirty windows, alters the speed of the passage of light. She refuses afternoon memories of neo-Gothic Italian vampire flicks, gossamer nightgown backlit by floods of filtered moonwash: the black stain between her legs. She's an insomniac, not a sleepwalker. A slender automaton of the dream seeking an unwary host, a red male fox.

Attention is everything. In the cold hallway, the decommissioned synagogue in Princelet Street, slide-projections splash the Lower East Side onto the wall. You scratch rendered New York twilight to reveal a phantom set of stairs. The dead were present all along. Fancy. How else could David Rodinsky have disappeared? Brick aperture thins to India paper skin. A migrant mob, poets and women, file out; take vodka against the clammy night air. The sky is blue as the underside of a lost tongue. A photographer, struggling for breath, captures his rival where he squats. An ancient taboo has been broken. Men in hats descend from the Ladies' Gallery. The senior witness, on the nod from the perfume of snuffed candles, warms himself on the lap of retrieved sound. The wings of his heart beat against a borrowed coat.

BELHAVEN

rasp with tongue the belly of an old wristwatch
whip your swift tongue around my wrist
smell like New York Times Square
like spit-chickens hotly
protesting kerosene butter slaughter, or
a black girl in leather with fur collar
stepping from the kerb at the junction of Restaurant Row
(where *Cats* is performed between bites) whispering
(no emphasis) 'wanna blow job?'
'what?' I say & she, undismayed, repeats it

the Paramount Hotel is underwater
drowned by Scientology coffee
made of dirt washed from Moloch gutters
yellow cabs illiterate between museums
Huncke's tropic hutch & Corso's clothes-strewn cabin
'hey man, don't take your shoes off'
til you know what Webster's Dictionary means by
'scryer' & Ed Sanders conducts the choir in a cold church
the heroically unlaved Mekas (J) whacked by cinema

a gerontocracy of privileged ghosts
preserved in close room Chelsea Hotels
tall views of an indifferent city
memory criminals parroting fortune cookie mantras
as snow blocks to wind river
banished smoke across Mafia bones
buried cock-in-mouth, industrial deadlands
where bright planes queue for their winter enema

NEARLY A MOON

no lounger to challenge the sea's reality
nice portion framed in a sellotaped porthole
bridal knots unpicked by sapient moonlight
as light frolics on impotent wavecrests
an ounce shy of the chair on the balcony

not *The Prisoner of Zenda* nor (most especially)
The Prisoner, air conditioning blown in Hotel Albion
3 fluorescent stars twinkle in an otherwise deserted
lobster tank, chalk blisters: 'successful' snaps are
the ones that go a tad out of focus
circumventing precision, here sharp here
betrayed by unpredictable human terrors, the old
poet stamps in off the cliffs, shaking rust from his beard
by wicket gate to encounter Charlton Heston Koo
Stark David Bailey &, inevitably, Dr Brian Hinton

Lear's daughters afloat in the salon
with Burmese princelings aggrieved
that spare ribs are off the menu
(& who's been generous enough to spare them?)
we sprawl & watch & wait the next kick of
salt spray spicing corset-coloured curtains
wondering what we've done to deserve
this delightful absence of phonecalls

CITY HEAT

ANGELS OF CHANCE

'Anything I can do, boss?' he asked.
'Watch this movie for me,' I said.
James Crumley

A crimson mouth smirks in his frosty forehead
steady increment of metropolitan desire, she suckles
the wrong stone, censoring first best thought
'That's what comes of working six months
in a bookstore on Madison Avenue.' Pavements
ill-suited to licensed heels, she spikes
the lazy voyeur's sporting eye. 'The eye altering
alters all.' 'Now,' she cries, 'now I understand.'
Sheer nakedness deposed as she lectures the chilling
stiff, not forgetting to flip her stitched collar to wink
at the blind doorman. 'Night, Charlie.' 'Night, Miss
Moonbeam.' Radon icepick flitched from
the scuppers of a Nantucket whaler spoils the line
of her pocket, uptown in illegitimate trenchcoat
bestowing custom on the yellowest cab in the universe

IRE-BOUND HOSE CO

'As men conveyed by witches through the air,
On violent whirlwinds!'
John Webster

Last night the witch came to me offering lampreys on iron,
wiggy skull-in-box, dusted gold, miming harm
& white as quicklime, shock'd to be alive, whispered shrieks
stood as if seated, lifeless living dead: sang
of 'clear blue water' which some call blood. Intelligencers
panders & orthodontists nervous in wings. Public friends grasp
angled elbow, restrain. Slick court-suits ensure succession

'Hell,' she declared 'is decommissioned, beyond scope
of privatisation. We would have it so.' Then homeless all,
herself unhoused & travelling by 1st-class cancer suite to
ordnance hotel. Train windows draped against intrusive lens.
Eyes mad as wingless sparrows. Wings are pearl
holsters to ration the irrational. Carrion blush,
she stoops to receive her vatic tribute

Ash in dormitory, documents on floor.
'Polypus of Roots of Reasoning Doubt'
adore bones that rattle in a metal cot:
bless the scar that never knew the whip.
She their corsair & their ship, vassel to vessel
gnaw greasy string, trust lanterns kept alight with
render'd human fat, rejoice for it, liberated
tundra. A mutton kingdom fit for dogs

REVENGE, LAUGHTER, PARADISE

Saved in salt, face partially crushed & drooping eye
scalds egg from skin in an over-occupied bedsit
dig the view book altar
occulted between shewstone & black candles
or check your ruin in an Aztec
obsidian mirror; set keel for fever islands
on a ticking couch, graceless garden plot, no
storyline (excess of script), history
the piss mark on an overnight bottle (analgesic
gum from shattered kidney dish)

Ed Kelly's retrieved fluid as tripod globe
vanishing blood ink
facilitates the storm, an invitation
grail cup
plays back, a shower of flawless light

books made holy by inscription, or vandalised by those
who assert an author's rite she can't
end with 'semen on his chin'. Sodden queen
presses lipstick print on cold marble
Stergene unknown, trilobyte domestica
gives head on the floor on wigs & feathers, not
with a running tap & a blind voyeur in attendance
ganging up against posthumous photographs
mouth silted in fearful intelligence

no room this in which to imagine what happens next

SNOW LIP

'For forgery, once, in Rutlandshire.'
Angela Carter

bird-creole or the billowing froth of bridesong
privately parsed & since unheard
from antechamber & dubious balcony caught
in bloody dew by sheet-examiners, rare
music to the sweaty hair-man who excuses himself
to boast piss & dip his scalded organ
in the athanor's cruel furnace

overlook a vitreous pier beyond which
the sea is hard as remembered fire
curvature like the alabaster arm of a Templar knight
who reaches across his sleepless pillow & cries
'touch me for our saviour's sake', kicking against
the lion stool that anchors his fretful soul

willing or not, the lake is artificial (as is her eye),
patterns of random magnetism
deform a church tower shattered by chopper blades
showy landing in the wrong field:
mortal diners lay aside their forks, await measurement
white suits & parasols, not grasping what *that* portends

ladies who lunch juggle plates
to disguise penile shavings of wet-pink fish
– bile grapes, snot balls, liver & lights -
take silver spoon & scoop the dripping clag
into the infanta's generous bodice

'nothing phases the river' he moans
drowning among liars' blackened teeth

WORLD'S OLDEST COMEDIAN IS DEAD

'Barbers are murdered in the night.'
                              Gregory Corso

Walking through wet wheat an ocean of mercury after
storm's head snapped in the wound
blunt spike driven deep into brain jelly: geography
of desire, sperm-tail photographed as galactic reduction
fetishes & footsore hyphens, delightful shoes,
neck-braces & mandrakes preserved in smoky bottles.
Disengage. Alchemy & the alchemist. Russian
in name only, sour silk drenched under coarse
serge, Comrade Commissar. 'Give us a twirl'.
Vile officer-class peons cowshit on their boots
perform in flawless French while swilling
wine glasses, best red, *fin* on scoped screen.
A word not a bite, signal to pull
back that gloved hand
from its almond oil trespass, tongue from cheek

It spells refreshed light outside the fire door shaken
into long coats, rain stalled, horn buttons undone
a loose belt, odd legs negotiating the cobbled slope
beneath an undistinguished church. Shark
in the shallows of a coffee-shop, mirrors everywhere
new underwear discreetly disclosed before
it is discovered (& distressed), golden
Muscat & another disappointing rhubarb *brûlée*
as preamble to permitted violation. Rime of a girl

in the doorway of a small hotel, thanking us for
not contributing to her relief, cocky Irishman
scoring a quid, hard coin, at the traffic lights
heraldic spoon twirling coffee rust to glacial sand

& then, & then again:
'My ignorance has been well preserved'

SERPENT'S TAIL TATTOO COMPULSORY

'His childhood...was hard. His family never ate deserts.'

Discretions of Chelsea, barrack grass no goats
fenced lawn your heavy drapes can certainly
keep the art at room temperature, shrapnel-gauze,
a quiet & patronising beneficence, dust-hour accurately
reflected in an Iris Murdoch novel. Freeze-dried virtue
defended connoisseurship entrain to leave
us feeling so sharp, contemplating another man's
good will: lunchtable treat for liver-spotted claws
veinless flesh, the river dull &
thick, pre-digestive reverie, taxi waved away.
How sexy the old man's limp, banknotes in boot.
Squid in ginger coaxes us back to adulterous heat,
afternoon rooms in which silence is a property value,
bookshops where they know how to package overseas
cabinets of watches saved from smoking battlefront
they do not tick, but whisper. Far across town, across wind-
tossed bridges & wastelots with Portakabins, a gross head
plastered pink to the wall. Curses born of tenderness,
invective, the snowy air-stream confederates
breath. He spits & swallows drool, glorying in
the surge of a fellow chancer's blood, lines of masks
the way he locates & humours aboriginal fault

The dull track through cancelled baptist temples
last street-market stalls Chaplin's memorial plaque
Babbage's prompt & who'd have guessed
there would be so many volumes buried beneath the Elephant's
flabby pink battlements when one is all it takes

THE FIFTH QUARTER

'He enjoyed a good view as long as he had his back to it.'
John Richardson

Once blueblack Velcro supported a wounded knee
once coral towers & speeding clouds
pain distinct as the taste of money
blade concealed in a layer of mashed prawn
now a blunt camera, a case more suited to deposition
a horse's head cast from noble blood line
a bowl of eels & veins laid with ceremony on the shore
just across the river from the new writers' pub

O feed me a fingernail of salt the magazine colours
of Abel Ferrara's *Cat Chaser* (please feed the cat)
storm foreplay, whirlwinds sucking up waves
something you notice at the horizon before the first
hit of fruit-burden'd sundowner: moist purple crab
pitting Hawaiian pyjamas, assaulting calico.
Addiction arrives with visiting card, fate announces
itself as a patch on your elbow, beware beware
the lozenge of chlorine the way light snakes
& dazzles. A couple of tequila slammers to windward
redundant actors, depilated, are hired to scoop
corn plasters from the liquid purity of the sky's mirror

& then, frugally, on a silver tray:
'the news of her death brought by a midwife'

MORE SPIT THAN POLISH

'Who prowls low-life pubs & eats woodcock for breakfast.'

chill Pils in Oxo / heady as
this morning's uric arc
Muscat with a crust on it, steamy
spout chewed in thick gristle-
flavoured bulbs of garlic

soft teaspoon gives up silver
til pink is reasserted on the curved
helmet of the cafetière, tracked
in transit to a double bedroom

the click of spit, chi released
by lazy spirals
of the sex act – ouch! *Les Homewreckers*
spring their disconcerting magick
baccy words in a wicked world, voice
like the cracking of gravestones

quite a sticky mess, actually
an honest man with a good hearing-aid
knows that journals are for journalists

ADDITIONAL AGENTS

'What sad things we become when warmth or wealth
tempts us from our natural gutters.'
Michael Moorcock

horn of plenty with bayonet warmth
tips in a plunge of regret for
lost opportunities the lack of a reliable camera

from stacked heights an exposed figure
far too good to last & the last of it, alas

chemical atlas in which protons sing
as city light bends & divides
the purity of an ankle-length dustcoat
caught on the wind, sightless hands
DON'T TOUCH, louche lad, arthritic paw
cozens the banister's invested heat

speckled water, roughed up, uncomplaining
a torpedo church with fired windows

blisters on the ball of the foot pop like seed pods
caressed air purrs, responding to
brown legs in animated shift
bodyweight on the pearl
now Camomile Street discloses: *a selection of*
evidence; maps; rantings; fragments; ephemera;
documents; traces; schemes; plans; collections etc

post office negotiations drag, bank art
the girl on the next stool but one, overcome
by matinal sunburst over church-roof, her white
drape vacancy across the back of a purposefully
uncomfortable chair, this unaligned border zone

so why are export cigars round not square?
the pirate exoticism of that shop, breath in jar
'a fetish for beauty'
the drone of a village explainer as loudly she
asserts the charm of paint-scored walls

Norton Rose: first a man & then a street

THE RIVER

A SERIOUS OF PHOTOGRAPHS
(RIVERWALK FROM THE ISLE OF GRAIN TO OXFORD)

hard on the heels of hope, westwards
unhyped, either bank 'could turn
into something or other' one pilgrim thinks
while his companion-----------------
is not recorded, no pocket scalpel to hack
through stubbled paddocks, a sense
of husbanded disease, soul fatigue, excess
vegetables, say it, baked beans
clouds of body gas to drop midges, open
land in a shame of underexploited air
always, to our right, the broad
& grumbling stream

ii

among the volume radiators pale
spines a library of dry & whistling pipes
bug overcoats – on foot you still
haunt urban attics – noise is kinder
(in the German sense) cannily
transported, red clay ridge, the bird
alights on a weak branch, holds its weight
waits, as we are too sudden & greedy
sighs, more shove less drive
out along the mud-crack'd shoreline
the rubber solution tide, bulk containers
trafficking pansy tubs on planks of shit

iii

In the 'first book-length study of the work' of J.H. Prynne the name of
Simon Armitage appears as frequently as that of Paul Celan. Discuss.

I don't for example consider that poets are
rock & roll old or new he
said apologetically quite the reverse
another case to drop from the carousel
duty declared & spoilt charms to ward off
the fear of flying fit nicely in a designer
carrier bag (later a bank mask & sex aid)
(later still a shield against nuclear sunburn)
so can you tell me the unident sneered
the nature of your business at the fibre optic
satellite of Gravesend (full marks for the
wall of early ripen'd figs), no answer as
our elevated cage swings out over the chalk
bowl the sepulchral stone of Dr Field

Kent 'rolling' eternally away. England
he gasped. Let's come back with a camera
as if we could, no chance of a teabreak
in Tel's roadside shack, the anachronistic
pick-up of the water tower, no trout
left in the pool. A lunchhour barmaid's
wren-brown neck is silently remarked,
high breasts, narrow waist, all that
artifice can add to nature. Ex-nautical

geezers in starched t-shirts & gold chains
out in the corn, the scarlet poppy pylon
dry fields where tide surges around a fixed post
& the noise of the dead is everywhere unheard

iv

in the hot field if you stand back to the willow
when our skiff locked & I tore open the
zip fitting cornflower blue remembered dress
emphasised by picnic basket & the death of our
unconscious sponsor a dwarf named Bill Shakespeare

in the cornfield standing in dust coloured coat
& taking breeze an oarsman's golden tent stubble
tight as the weave of a cat's belly the spectre who
sometimes scratches at our varnished door

nice kinship with cloud flight distinct
outline of Sinodun clump your shadowfall
to calculate lost time: *river's over there*

a current reverie passes between two
photographs the seizure not between us
I am redundant to what occurs which is
where the track directs itself back
towards the Thames & if your sleeves
are an inch or so too short then
so much the better your arms strength I
exploit elsewhere & am eager to unload

v

I burned the beast hut
hurting the huge
ah ghosts ah money

please pass either side

WHITE GOODS
(2002)

'Surely the force that had overwhelmed all the rest of the world would have little trouble snuffing out a last ragged band of hold-outs in London's East End. And after that?'

K.W. Jeter

'Then the boat drew alongside Tilbury pier. The first building we saw on the waterside was one of those huge hotels, all stucco and pinnacles, which stare from the English coast like idiots staring over an asylum wall.'

George Orwell

'A man's stride betrays whether he has found his way: behold me walking.'

Nietzsche

WALKING UP WALLS

for Jock McFadyen

Woke up this morning.

Pain, that bright corkscrew, twisting the spine. A green thing ahead of me. A fibre optic rope. And instead of Long John's parrot, a packet of icy peas perched on my frozen shoulder. Tendons, arteries, veins: melded into bone. Pectoral girdle. Home is a foxhole, a remembered hedge.

 On the move, early, exorcising an undefined horror. Watching pale shoe-leather change colour, dewy meadow fragrant with dog shit. ATAQUE GRAVE. AS A MUGGER YOU ARE NEVER SAFE. It doesn't matter who you are, who you think you are, the trick is: never, *ever*, stay still.

Substantial portions of Hackney were missing. Missing from my memory. Concrete slabs. Floating envelopes of dust. Negatives of lost buildings. Period debris. If we can't retain those monoliths, what hope? Ambulatory amnesia. Details - stains, cobbles, weeds, pub signs - faded, shifting. Removed. Absent. What hope? How shall I recover my identity? What identity? My purpose. Not me, nor him. Now then.

Walking is forgetting. Shrugging off fear, the loss of a self no longer required. I walked east; a shocked face hopeful of sunlight, rumours of warmth. Loose head too big for its cradle. Mare Street a necessary hiatus, more than a ditch, less than a highway. A collision of cultures and aborted aspirations. Fire-damaged *Indochine Brasserie*. Silver lettering against carbonized damage. A pair of giant spectacles with ice-blue eyes.

I thought: take Mare Street. Somebody has to. I'd never seen it before, not like this. Take it for a long ride. Arrows painted on the ground: cycles, green paths, officially sanctioned routes. They're trying to tell me something, I said, swinging away, heading south. Left arm dangling, useless as a length of tarry twine. I was one of the unsanctioned cripples, without a motorised buggy and a parking permit.

The Picture Palace. Vanished. I remembered razor fights, rucks. Brylcreem and French letters. Reading about them in ghosted gangland memoirs. I remembered political slogans, obscenities. Shuttered windows curtained in corrugated sheeting: the building was a reservoir of dreams. Sugary secretions. Glucose and semen blistering ancient velour. Now it was an empty frame. Beams of blue light from an archival past, cinema-smoke polluting present indifference. Voices of the dead. 'Harry made seventy pounds a tube - he ran the business.'

Unpremeditated pedestrianism ameliorated the pain, shifted it into the sinews of the city; a red sweat of disregarded signage, buses, kebab-house neon. STRIPTEASE glows above a votive garden, burns through a heavy collar of leaves. Walking is forgetting. An urban guide, a fantastic map of Hackney, duplicated the island outline of Britain. Everything unmanifest. Lost in dark cloud. Until Turner's Road meets Ackroyd Drive.

Adjacent to canal and railway, near the stadium. Urban dreaming. They were good names, Turner, Ackroyd. I brushed them off my mildewed sleeve, bird-shit. Pick one, a name. Pick a story, a life.

Wincing in a public garden. Or, at any rate, holding myself upright on an open gate. Regulated beds, grim rows. The frost, melting, gifted small cabbage-like purple plants with an crystalline glitter. Neither one thing, I thought, nor the other. Neither flower nor veg. Not ice, nor water. Between states of being. A quiet flux.

What we see is what other people have forgotten. *Keep going.* Move fast enough to access the stillness, the times when strangers pause, see something out of the window, a landscape bent around the curvature of wind-streaked glass. What is not loved is what remains.

The A13 is a lucky road; in this early light, splintered, engorged by blood-mess. A Turner infusion. Liquid gold. Like a drench.

The veins stood out in my shoulder. You could see a nest of them pulsing beneath the cheap jacket. Out here, the missing squares of the map didn't matter. Everything was missing. Everything was transitional, hoardings transformed luxury goods - by a system of revolving panels - into obtrusively-breasted young women. Real buildings, ex-industrial, were less convincing than the replicas: deserts, oceans, gas stations in New Mexico. A post-nuclear clarity. Fault lines radiating out from monster boards onto the camber of the road. *The desert is coincidence between the beginning and the end.*

The exhibition of the world: interventionism. A permanently temporary museum. A drive-through wonderland of leather sofas and disassembled shelf units, warehouses of empty shoes, gleaming golf clubs. Public art in landscape format. Anonymous masters labouring for our entertainment: smoking cowboy horsemen, cars that drive themselves, lean brown torsos lacking body hair.

Pick a name, a fresh identity. *Warner. McDonald. Ford.* Think of yourself as Harry Dean Stanton, Joel McCrea, Neville Brand. Malign shadows of Chinook helicopters over Beckton Alp. A war zone soundtrack. I'll readdress myself, I improvised, to Gillette, Wyoming. Sharp as a razor my blunt reflexes.

Up on those fairground ramps, by the three pink towers, the A13 becomes the credit sequence of *The Sopranos*. 'Woke up this morning'. Wet cigar. Water tower. Elbow resting on the padded lip of the open window. I clocked TV in a Vietnamese takeaway. That's what I took away, moving images. A song. *Reached for my gun*. The A13 was East London's homage to New Jersey, the empty bits, out beyond the airport, where hoodlums buried guys with severed cocks in their mouths.

Retail landfill. Cinemascope-sized chunks of nothing. The only way to access this shit was to walk along the rim of the inhabited world with a visor-shaped hole cut from a black rubbish bag, a hood on the head.

The sky was too full, a bowl of blotting-paper roses. Striding out, as if I should, half a day into this thing, catch up with the shadow that was always ahead of me. As if I should, finally, come to understand why all these bites had been removed from my memory, from the topography. The road ghosted the river. It had taken over the river's function, bearing its traffic, dirt cargoes. Traduced immigrants travelling blind in sealed containers. What do they hear? How do they imagine the skin of this place?

Something was missing, the pain. It was sucked out of my shoulder into glinting, tin-coloured rivulets, into off-highway retail parks, burger furniture. The McDonald's logo read like: *M for Mammal*. Like cone breasts dispensing acid milk. A triumphal arch for Baghdad. A devastated Garden of Eden.

Cars. I began to notice abandoned cars. Non-wrecks. Partial wrecks with spider-web windows. POLICE AWARE. That's what the filth do, these days, put out notices. They'll flash you for moving too fast. Stop you if you're cruising through the city in the wrong motor, the wrong tan factor. Transport above your station. Otherwise, it's all PR. Sign-writing. WARNING. COVERT OPERATIONS TAKING PLACE IN THIS AREA. POLICE ROBBERY INITIATIVE. Cars deserted because they ran out of petrol. Joy riders out of love with their borrowed wheels. A fiercer loop. Petty thieves of Bow and Poplar and Forest Gate won't cross the M25, they won't break the circuit.

A chalk quarry, evening. A stopping point, if not a destination. The chalk is a wall of canvas. A breakers' yard of missing images. Paintings that died in the heroic attempt to duplicate landscape, to pin down shifting discriminations of light. Spoiled pinks, rotten cadmium. Old Hackney. Painted walls leaning against actual walls. Paintings with thumb prints and heel prints, walked-over canvases. Suspension bridges that were projected photographs. Immutable metamorphoses.

That's it then, I decided. All there is. Either you walk the pain or you freeze it; freeze yourself, go into the thing you are watching. The painter had got away. The paintings remained, roadside hoardings disguising other versions of themselves, multiples. Holes everywhere. And this was the pit where movement met silence.

My neck went into spasm. I couldn't write. My arm wouldn't lift. Wind from passing traffic puffed the canvases into sails. The paintings billowed and bellied. No collaboration was possible. Language contradicts the pure information of layered paint. The painter was fucked. I was fucked, the city was fucked. Memory a sentimental indulgence. Whatever is sold, or offered for sale, becomes another word for money. So that's it, I said. That's why these paintings are shaped like cheques. Like the windscreens of American cars. Like the space between quotation marks. They're not much, when you set them against the transcendent weirdness of the road, this territory. But they're all we've got. And we're lucky to have them. If we do. When we do. When we pay attention.

WHITE GOODS

'I can still run in a straight line'
                    Mark Wright

day special so ordinary plain birds
throb & are overruled the rip of sky

seams of burnt air *I've started so I'll*
choose to abandon where space inside

the body is darkness he says printed
defacing as it shapes the ruled page

leasing sea its horizonal vertigo
the privilege of scoring the beat

breathless & overexposed in white
runs of smoke leaking from our

sawdust man good woman's cup
'disgust' shapes her narrowed lips

burgled by life the riotous candle
devours its own pink fat

designer collars for slaves &
willing subterraneans stript of fur

mercury is a step too far he denies
the twist in bone the dying yellows

OBSCENERY OF THE EAST

for Chris Torrance

walking to where there is no weather
bits of my head, whispering
doesn't ease it, or the lurid continuum

of shadows across mattress grass
the raven's fee, believe me
breath like piss runs downhill

Wick Wood futured now
cropped in thistle & blowweed
maggot-flies in place of butter

nothing shines with more novelty than
a slack isthmus the resting bicycle
tomorrow they know won't be as fine

GUIGNOL'S BAND AID

'The only real thing about her was her false leg'
J. H.

folded children
upon whom old biddies gaze
pointing unshocked in mock surprise
the hollow wooden clack of girl-heels
referencing chalk encrustations, bright scars
of the no longer white house, a fishy
odourless sky trenched with pressure
pylons carrying thin blue souls east
down the flagged canal
I had always imagined
no more poetry no libraries

sailing proud
dust-lilies on petrol water

PULHAMITE GROTTO IN SILVERTOWN

i.m. Francis Stuart

Among stone ear fractures night
applies its cold shawl to the indifferent
mass of Kensington: awls, owls
he listens - they're stuffed, granite &
calcite & red radicals / sparkle
he's a brown bomb, dumb for redemption
crophaired, stalking deserted marble
halls; calling rivers, state-sponsored
hideouts in Canning Town, under future
flightpaths. In the elective rubble shredded
breath whispers *Madeleine*, someone
to betray - unbandage my foot, recall
imperial measures, she gorges in greenhouse
volcanic ash. The generosity (affable &
unconsidered) of a metropolitan Jew:
come back come back, too late to court
greywet skies, the priest hole & your
father's interminable suicide. That's
time, that's sand that's sun, put a packet
on the wrong nag. 'That's right'

Geology has no truck with leaking parcels
soft estates or wayward Irish lives

BECKTON ALP

Cycle with Jock and hear the past told. Pylons gates cemeteries under a big sky. You smell burnt rubber, not the shit. Flood of London's waste. You're high. On the Ridgeway. Head in clouds. Jock remembers: dirt-tracking, early tape, his kids. The immaculately leathered youth, who stunted on the slope, outdid them all. On his one arm and specially adapted bike. Remembers sub-teens on the A13, unlicensed, catching the slipstream. Remembers Will Self's description of how his Volvo 'bent' into metalled curves. Remembers crushing oil cans for employment. The fiction of Scotland.

The point of a good view is that it should capture, and give relief from, the journey that led up to it. There are no good views in isolation. No empty frames. Unwalked, uncycled. Unearned. View is always an accident, a breathing space.

Walking the pilgrim path of Joseph Bazalgette's Northern Outfall Sewer, slantwise to the south-east, brings the traveller - if he times it right, afternoon, late in the season - up against the glorious absurdity of the Beckton Alp. A conical mound that can be ascended by a sequence of zigzag paths (resting places thoughtfully provided). The gentle climb, this compromise between human and mountain-bike gearing, allows time for the weary pedestrian to warm-down before the summit. He can play back the drift along the outflow, the brutally hacked verges, bright-blue benches, the mustard brickwork (serviced by miscreants for the next generation of spray-can bandits).

Memory is a wound.

A pointlessly exotic pumping station. Channelsea Creek with its anachronistic mudlarks dredging for sovereigns (in an age of post-Orwellian gameshows). Cancer hymns in low-slung cables. Our brains fried by electronic overload, idiot conversations in an acoustic meadow.

The click of the wheel that works the empty ski-lift mechanism. Traffic on an arterial road. Scimitars of sunlight flashing on windscreens. We were here for the eclipse. Jock is here now in his dark glasses. My great-grandfather crossed the Andes on a mule.

By and by the heart's action seemed to fail, and I suddenly collapsed, slipped off the saddle and lay down on my back, my mule gasping for breath beside me. When I gradually came to myself, I could see around me the bones of many a good mule and llama, cleanly picked, while high in the air floated the ever alert condor, said to be the largest and most powerful of all birds; but I was not just then in a mood to admire his proportions nor appreciate his attentions, and, gathering myself together again with the help of a more fortunate companion, I moved on, but only for fifty yards, when I again fainted. This was repeated at least fifty times till the crest was crossed and some progress was made down the western slopes.

The summit has it all. The pulse of an orange sun dissolves an unreal city, Canary Wharf and Docklands. Golden browns of Stanley Kubrick's imposed paddy fields, the old Beckton gas works as Vietnam. Jock dirt-tracked around the perimeter of the set. *Full Metal Jacket.* Flaring, scarlet brake-lights on Newham Way. Levels and counter-levels of traffic, hot for the estuary, heading home to dormitory estates on the rim of chalk quarries.

This site is mythic, aligned with the lost mound of Whitechapel, the undiscovered culture of Silbury Hill. It's the best kind of fake. It aspires to the language of television. Skiing for motorists. A rubber carpet with the texture of a Little Chef waffle. The commodification of transcendence. Black smoke, thick with sugar droplets, from Tate & Lyle's Silvertown factory.

Leaning on a creosoted railing, London makes sense. There is a pattern, a working design. And there's a word for it: *Obscenery.* Blight. Stuttering movement. Distant river. The time membrane dissolves, in such a way that the viewer becomes the thing he is looking at. Jock's glasses reflect meltdown: dual carriageways, ramps and run-offs in two panels. Green rays of the setting sun strip flesh from the bone. He's done it, vanished into a Ludwig Meidner apocalypse, an epic painting with an intensity he knows he will never achieve. So he settles for representation, bricks and mortar. The artist is redundant. As is the reporter. The photograph. The memory prompt. Useless. We're still on the inside of the outside, searching for cracks. Trapped in an envelope of tired flesh. View is raw and absolute and unappeased.

PARROT TAROT

'bogus mendicants Parsifal muff'
                    John Wieners

rain is a solid / seal the cupboard
where rubberized lengths play havoc
with weak eyes, knees creak & genuflect
before the ravelling tongue can scroll fur
& filth, genetic telgrams, flush
bulge to seepage bite, swallow that raw
mess you carry away on the afternoon's
increasingly desperate quest, better now?

the Xerox'd building skims Portland contracts
memory skein, salt crystals, a funerary wrap
headlines printed on hot white chips, dog lard
in fact: I AM THE M25 KILLER

THE KONIGSBERG BRIDGE PROBLEM

fly by night
& vulture-priest by day
woman always / my red poppy
bursts from the dump. answer
the river, please
in quick strokes polish the ship's bawd
with Krakow vinegar ward off moonfat
scene-stealers solitary canoodling
among drowned powder boats
humpbacked predators of the shallows
one man jumped flaming into water & lived
the other choosing grass was flambéed

a lizardly solution
a blackstone plate

NICE BLOOD

in late sky sheep float
soaked with saline
memory-fleece the river
tastes of tea: we will all die
frequently hopelessly but
the yard crop still flowers in saffron
& sweet tobacco herbs split
sharp tiles, wide the measure
of moisture high sky mirrored
in a droplet jewel pinned to
pierced breast, then back
steaming to tin mug & crust, kneel
before you rise, wet with rumour

FROM THE THICK END OF A PURFLEET TELESCOPE

Notes in advance of Chris Petit's film, *The Carfax Fragment*

Tell them to take off the strait-waistcoat. I have had a terrible dream.

Unstable metaphors. Energy inertia flow.

One image, following immediately upon another, discloses a third: as something strange and previously unimaginable.

IMMIGRATION. STORAGE. DISTRIBUTION.

Everything happens in threes. Water sand tarmac. Blood diesel light. The director Don Siegel's first job was cutting sunsets into sunrises.

We have of late come to understand that sunrise and sunset are to her times of peculiar freedom.

Michael Reeves, a disciple of Siegel, killed himself - by accident or design - at the age of 25. His first feature was a vampire story. *Revenge of the Blood Beast.*

Count Dracula shelters in a suicide's tomb.

Brown sea leeched of life. The colour of dried blood. Joseph Conrad and Bram Stoker. Waiting on a sluggish tide. A craft with no crew, under full sail. Toxic ballast. Aliens. The undead of Margate. Feared asylum-seekers: gypsies, Romanians. Garlic-chewers terrified of garlic. Nosferatu in the form of a black dog or crow. *Polyglot - very polyglot - polyglot with bloom and blood.*

Blood, for asylum-seekers, is a commodity. When all else fails, sell a kidney.

When a metaphor 'takes' - an inoculation, a nicotine patch - landscape never recovers. Downriver Purfleet, by Stoker's curse (copyright 1897), is always Dracula's abbey. The poisoned shoreline is his garden. Carfax, the fictional name for his estate, is prophetic: CAR/FAX. Unmanned container ships loaded with the multiples of Dagenham. Herded together like Victorian criminals, automobiles are faxed into the Third World. Van Diemen's Land. Metal news, funeral barges.

Carfax, a place where four roads meet. The traditional burial pit, stake through heart, of a vampire. John Williams, the supposed Ratcliffe Highway Murderer, was buried, as De Quincey reports, at the junction of Cannon Street Road and Cable Street. In the shadow of Nicholas Hawksmoor's St George-in-the-East. One hundred yards from the legendary distribution centre of (book-running ghost) Nicholas Lane; antiquarian rarities, cocaine. The brilliant sunrise-yellow of a first edition of Stoker's *Dracula*, titled in scarlet.

Names are viruses. They are immortal. Dr John Seward, Stoker's lunatic asylum keeper, helps to christen the 20th-century poet of addiction: William Seward Burroughs. Metaphors of viral invasion, AIDS fantasies, infected blood. Blood as fuel. Stored blood. Diesel blood. *Seward will cut off his head at once and drive a stake through his heart.*

The present plagiarises the past. Stoker's vampire is Dreyer's *Vampyr*, is Murnau's *Nosferatu*. Mrs Stoker, Bram's widow, initiates law suits. Max Schreck is an animate X-ray, a parodic Jew in a racist fable. Prince of the Ghetto. Returned to Bremen to begin the story afresh. Import/export. Culture cargoes. Festival fodder. Vampirised images shot for the second time.

When I came back to Purfleet with a cameraman and sound-recordist, we walked the river path from Grays on a morning of high, scudding clouds, rapidly-advancing weather fronts. A displaced person, a Canvey Island fisherman, remembered: 'a river of soles.'

IMMIGRATION. STORAGE. DISTRIBUTION.

Floating across the sky, juggernauts obey the laws of early-modernist Imagism. Burroughs' metaphor: diesel-blood, petroleum jellies. Wilhelm Reich. The cab of the lorry is an orgone accumulator. *WR, Mysteries of the Organism.* Soixante-neuf. The sexual politics of storage tanks, tubes, pistons, machinery. Robot sex behind razor-wire fences.

William Burroughs is both doctor and vampire, Van Helsing and Dracula. The face of the century. A water mask. A face turned inside-out. A winged helmet.

I got a cup of tea at the Aerated Bread Company and came down to Purfleet by the next train.

Ladders. Walkways. Spider-runs. The storage facility, the distribution centre is the vampire's castle.

ESSO. S/O. Stoker's Oracle. Among the glistening storage tanks, shadows slithering across windowless boxes, you will find the residue of Dracula's abbey. The pilgrim church in the overgrown garden.

Hauliers protesting price rises, fuel duties, picket the Purfleet depot. Blood/oil. The air is scented. Plants are unnaturally plump. Meat-fed. Procter & Gamble's soap factory is Dracula's castle. Miraculously blue concentration-camp flowers. White vestments, rags caught on wire. Soap made from human fat.

Smoke, steam, condensation. The restless dead travel as smoke. Forming and reforming. Scripting a debased landscape. Smoke as code. Papal elections. Incineration of surgical dressings.

The mist grew thicker and thicker... I could see it like smoke - or with the energy of boiling water...it became concentrated into a sort of pillar of cloud...through

the top of which I could see the light of the gas shining like a red eye.
Perimeter fences protect heresies, alchemical experiments. The white pulp of trashed libraries. Stoker and Stevenson and Conrad. Rotting in bales. Books that have been drowned, rather than burnt.

Dracula, when his name is spoken in chinese whispers, with a South African accent, becomes 'Dreck Cola.' DISTRIBUTION. Dross on the move. Landfill: the only traffic on the river.

Hieroglyphic entries in thick, half-obliterated pencil... the destinations of the boxes. There were, he said, six in the cartload which he took from Carfax and left at 197 Chicksand Street, Mile End New Town, and another six which he deposited at Jamaica Lane, Bermondsey. If then the Count meant to scatter these ghastly refuges of his over London, these places were chosen as the first of delivery, so that later he might distribute more fully.

DRACULA plc. Dracula franchise. A multinational operation. Transylvanian earth. Spores hidden in sand. Sand fountains. STORAGE. DISTRIBUTION. Legoland houses. Seward's asylum converted into Wimpey homes, rabbit-hutch units.

A motorway policeman pulls up alongside us. 'You know you can't cross over.' The QEII Bridge is forbidden to pedestrians. You are permitted to stand in the cycle lane, to watch south-flowing traffic. Sunlight glinting on windscreens. Surveillance auditions. Stopovers for sales reps. Double-glazing. Mormon motels.

Reverse the film and revise history. Left is right. Rivers become roads. The working Thames is now the circuit of the M25. Immigration is re-cut as emigration. It's an editing decision. Wind-surfers are revealed as Dracula's victims, his henchmen: prophylactic uniforms, skin suits, anti-viral protection. *Judex.* Cocteau's outriders. The undead as bad weather Californians. Escaping. Riding the storm.

All that die from the preying of the Un-Dead become themselves Un-Dead, and prey on their kind. And so the circle goes on ever widening, like as the ripples from a stone thrown in water ... nosferatu, as they call it in Eastern Europe ... and would make more of those Un-Deads that have filled us with horror.

SOS: CARFAX

the small (wooden)
boat of memory
container ship submerged hulk
sliding down a rule of sludge cereals
M25 as target logo
battery to barrier
surrogate cloud pilgrimage
less formal than
the first funeral less fun than
a wake: soapsmoke backache
retired sunlight
scintillating on old water

SLOOZE

'They weren't all fascists. Some of them were crypto-fascists.'
Michael Moorcock

peel the onion sky over Purfleet black
oil inside blue lid: Neruda's TV
impersonator by pink house
making fruitskin into meat trim: my daughter
speaks of simulated blood, tomato & treacle
all I want from landscape is to be left alone
the warmth of touch on a white eye
& time retrieved from blank screen
language-hurt padded with a lost ocean

SNAPSHOTS FOR ROBINSON
(DARTFORD TO GRAVESEND)

1. On a ridge above the Dartford Crossing, the
   Sakis Hotel. A venue favoured by U.S.
   evangelists and operated entirely by slot-
   machines. *Sunday Brunch £16.95. 3 Course
   Carvery & Jazz Band. Eat as Much as You Can!*

2. CROSSWAYS. Giant letters in retail park.
   An informal plantation of pylons.

3. Robinson approves the architectural vernacular
   of Dartford: windowless boxes. The coming,
   off-highway aesthetic: neutrality. Absence
   of signature. *Asda Backs British Beef.*

4. *Ambient Goods Inward.* Stopped roads where
   container-transporters park. Limbo zones of
   rubbish. Verges soured with plastic.
   Improvised culinary and sexual transactions.

5. Ingress Abbey. Devasted mud. A building site.

6. Graffito on river wall: *Thatcher Out!*

7. The cranes and hoists of Northfleet. Under a
   heavy sky, Robinson eating a banana. A snail
   hanging from a spear of wet grass.

8. *Pelican Fabrications. Seacon Terminals Limited. Britannia Refined Metals. London Coaches. Flat-Out Karting. Thames Timber.*

9. The locked stadium of Dartford and Northfleet F.C.

10. A wall of figs in a Gravesend industrial estate.

11. A chalk quarry. Not yet converted into a second Bluewater. Robinson suffers from vertigo.

12. A fibre optic colony. Guarded by a lighthouse, topped with concrete water tank.

13. Graffito on tile wall: *Eat the Establishment.*

14. A microphone, on a tripod, placed on a traffic island.

15. A chaplet of sunflowers woven into a chainlink fence. *Warning Guard Dogs On Patrol.*

16. The Gravesend-Tilbury ferry: *Princess Pocahontas.*

CHINESE BOXES

'the next film for the late Louis Malle'

the director sniffing yellow
empty 'small cigar' box that
carries his name paper nostalgia
for those nights German women &
bitter coffee lime avenues monitor
screens blizzarded in grain now
declines with regret this opportunity
to review a novel in which his name
real & invented features
a video collector who snorts plastic
cases extinguished pain
the red & the marmalade
shield against traffic haze adulterated
life stock when bad times
made for good poetry

SADDLING THE RABBIT
(2002)

'That our memory, which is our self, is tiny limited and fallible, is also one of the most important things about us, like our inwardness and our reason. Indeed it is the very essence of both.'
Iris Murdoch

TASSELS, BLUEBEARDS & PLASTER CHEESECAKE

BUSINESS LOVE

wax elephants of Whitechapel
glycerine pearls they sit

in cabinets proud, fat
haunches spreadeagled

brewers' creature brewer's droop
his weeping eye, trophy & sediment

glitter-trash transcendence:
the quest for a better battery

GAUDY LIVERS

'It was the hour between dog and wolf, as they say.'
                                                    Jean Rhys

Fournier Street, dusk is absolute, outside
black-pink lips of the Jesus fountain
waterless in an external passage, twin silver
pen-feathers pinch the breast,
primed with venom, love darts to lubricate
the young husband Mauritian, apron'd
stewer of fish scales, warty appendages
          Skull suckers! Shiteaters! Millionaires!
you pick lint from the drain of colonised
corduroys, mustard & horsewhips
bugger me how that German talks his green
heresy flight from paper, the coins
he planted in an earlier life. Youth plucked
from Streatham chicken shack, sleepless
street dancing with passover truckers, HGV
men & licensed halal butchers, scabs
beneath black bra straps itch & fester

Creased dawn flagging a bloody cityscape
they batten down the hatches, activate the
answerphone &, camera in hand, set out
in search of strong tea & fresh birdshit

ROOM SERVICE DECLINED

'Memory is a wound'
                    Jochen Gerz

The brokering of secret spaces. Poets haunt the purlieus of the city in direct competition with developers, real estate pirates. They practice the same black arts. They operate, after the mouthwashes and the colognes, as franchised psychics; mediums tapping erased myths, fixing inverted commas around a previously innocent terminology: *the room, the arch, the loft, the vault.* Latex gloves over hairy knuckles, heavy-gold signet ring pricking a bent pinky.

Princelet Street drifts. The story we had to tell is no longer required. The former synagogue has become a charity case. Its business: the acquisition of public funds, imposed and obedient versions of the past. Nicholas Hawksmoor's carpenter, dead Huguenots, multicultural display cabinets.

Walks then, inspired by markings found in the hermit's tanned and friable *London A-Z.* A city faded and dusty as the posthumous map. Nicotine paper impregnated with the disappeared man's spirit, his reluctant breath. Phlegm of green rivers. Hair-sweat of conceptual excursions. *He would compulsively pace up and down, or in circles, always clockwise. He had an obsessive conviction that he should put the whole world, and the heavens and angels, in his head, or in his heart.* The map becomes that heart; venturing into its channels, we are lost. We lose ourselves. False starts, misunderstood evidence.

The interesting aspect was the afterburn. How other people, unknowns, followed the hermit's trail: recording sound, making compositions from columns of words in broken books. They undertook pilgrimages to compensate for their failure to gain access to the synagogue. The room had been cleared, drained of essence and meaning. 'Just because you can't see a thing,' said Ed Dorn, 'it doesn't mean that it's no longer there.' (Sentiments soon to be echoed in a top dollar BMW promo.) Let dust settle on the tongue. The bell is quilted in pigeon lime. And it costs £40 to climb the church tower.

A Swiss-based architect, sharpwitted and free to travel on a regular basis between Zurich and London, begins her quest in Spitalfields. Digital camera, laptop. Hand luggage. Love letters - the affair ended badly - found in a skip. She records a conversation in which a 'facility fee' for a visit to the 'improved' attic is set at £2,000. So she constructs, elsewhere, her own version of this place, 'a memory for the absent body'.

Angry machines scratch patterns of powder from the wall. Photosensitive plates fix ambulant shadows and plot the transits of the conjured presence.

Later, the lessons of her early improvisations absorbed, the architect finds herself at the point where the faint red line on the hermit's map loses its nerve and breaks off. A complex motorway interchange, with a life of its own (horses, scrubland, radio masts, CCTV cameras), sits at the foot of the hill where the hermit's sister died in a monstrous asylum colony. The architect doesn't climb the hill, thereby denying herself the lift of an unexpected view back down to Docklands and the river. She isn't interested in narrative neatness, stories with proper endings. She conceives, instead, in her modesty and arrogance, her innocent ambition, a museum of memory. *I want to climb into his skin.*

Buried sensors monitor traffic flow, affecting the fabric of this never-to-be-built building, influencing pilgrim dreamers in their alcoves of incubation. Purity. Ritual baths. Noise filtered into intelligent units, mantic and familiar. The walls are thin as India paper, thick as the masonry of the Tower of London. They act as 'a weight or an anchor for the retreat'. And in this retreat walkers advance into the universal past. Nobody makes a charge for something that isn't there. White ghosts in the trees on the hill are unappeased. Estate dwellers, behind ornate ironwork gates, are otherwise engaged. Movement of traffic on the road, stuttering, frustrated, is the only absolute. End of endlessness. The beginning of acceptable ignorance.

CONTINUOUS SKY

for Lee Harwood

> *'the artist's general disposition to vibrate'*
> Henry James

a lightgreen coat moves commonly east, un-
inspired, but up for it, a shifty sky with its rouge theatre
stacked in golden curls, cold enough for fingerless gloves, can
you believe 'The Poet' is now a wine bar in Mitre Street & how does
'6 Irish Oysters with soda bread' (at £7.80) grab you? or
'Seaweed cured Salmon' (at £5.50) backed by a slab of good
Galway taybreadandbutter? the poet is effortlessly divorced
from the poem (like the abuser from mother church). no
solitaries with red notebooks, no silver paint like Stephen
Rodefer's decadent nails. business folk (women included)
drip chardonnay on small round tables. yellow & blue
they have decided will stand as poetry's flag

the motif offers coherence to a fragmented cityscape,
with many obstacles for pedestrians to surmount, keeping
the trek interesting: hurdle fences, tarmac'd mud
carbonized angels in dim recesses, Byzantine tesserae glinting
blood & rubies, unredeemed nimbuses, the run to Cable Street
hobbled, minor league Minories, and it hits me, flashing
to the back story, that 'poet' is another way of saying 'Irish',
twisted window-slats that were once blind, only in the
Square Mile are churches heated & open (incensed): *Ralph
Clay Esq of Hackney Who in the 65th Year of his Age
closed an honourable and useful Life*

browse nautical charts before swinging left to where
the Seaman's Library used to stand on the corner of
Dock Street, now as you rightly suppose Ludlow Thompson
Residential Sales, blue (again) & old gold (yellow), one-bedroom
apartments of the type that might once have seemed, under
white emulsion, desirable to romantics who read French verse
& liked to blend Gauloises, goat curry and sewage outflow
from the foreshore, Supremes on the jukebox and the
mythical hooting of tugboats on the Thames, all bollocks
like imported sand making a Southend of Tower Bridge.
nothing has gone that was ever here. freakish ceramic cod
the dive with the movie star collages & the sign that leads
the discerning stalker to Wilton's Music Hall with its
astonishing pink door, pomegranate & pineapple panels
the deep eros of purple impinging on blushing labia: BIG
LOVE. shuttered to the blarney screech of Fiona Shaw
emoting the lifeblood out of *The Waste Land*. 'the phrases
of the afternoon, or early morning,' he wrote, 'finally do
make a life full turn.' quiet vortices of Bengali kids, post-
economic migrants, unschooled in Wellclose Square, are
shepherded towards asymmetrically lit tower blocks, cloud-
shavings soluble in the still water of the memorial font.
bright chatter, long black coats swishing against the pull
of the L. bones skulls books deals compasses confectionery
loud as third world toothpaste, hospital mosque poverty
pit. getting holding moving on, coming, coming back none
the worse for what has been attempted & abandoned, risk
knowing & not knowing, never knowing when &
why to turn on your heel, switch off, go home

BURNT POLAROIDS & UNNOVEL NOVELLAS
OF URBAN DISPENSATION

A PAINTER CALLED MILTON

i.m. the film-maker MK

receipt the work of a life uncorrected proof
cold custard with pinch of coffee essence
strobing tubed light so this
is how we come to it a rush
at the false stair spectacles spilled
lens loose detached cornea convexing
ceiling world breath lost pulse stopped
you made the *Potemkin* reference & recalled
a Kensington gardens pram bumping as
you crawled from the paper swamp plates
clapped to your temples fried hair scrolled
tongue too heavy for mouth blue lead
tipping back drowned skull dragging at
stiff heels squeezing your chest cavity
'deader than dead' the eye-witness reported
crossing towards the Goodge Street *Pret à Manger*
hand frozen in air for one instant before
patting a red hydrant problem solved rain-breeze
the search for some compensatory token
Option Click by Dave McKean: the way we were

MR MOORCOCK IS NOT EXPECTED

'returning became more difficult'
Jim Dodge

An unequal contest. 12th January, 2001. Royal Courts of Justice. Regina vs. Michael John Moorcock. The jurist William Blackstone - in whitestone - gripping a textless marble book. Ghosts of the law, up on their plinths. High security, lazily enforced. No cameras allowed, unless they are trained on you. There is a molecule-bombarding division between street and court. Crims and lawyers are distinguishable by their tailoring. (One dressed down, shabby-black with polished shoes - and the other done up like a dog's dinner, brutal colognes failing to override fear-sweat).

Eyes. The way daylight catches trauma when they step outside, into sunshine, towards microphones and taxis. You don't enter that hall, unless you have some business - even if that business is idle curiosity. The street shivers: a zebra crossing that seems to stretch as far as the QEII Bridge. Stymied smokers in tight conclaves, awkward in occasional suits.

They're here: Bow, Bethnal Green, Cable Street, Plashet Road, Plaistow. They've been let in: lowlifes with orange (cordial-stain) hairpieces, ponytails knotted like old tars, ducktail anachronisms. But crims don't do anachronism. They are fixed in man-and-boy tradition, inherited fashion. Larging it. Want to see flares, waistcoats, limegreen linings, sovereign rings? Come to the Royal Courts of Justice. Shaven heads, neck tattoos, Peter Wyngarde moustaches: they concentrate, as much as they can, repeat the story, under the tuition of pouchy-eyed young women. They yawn, the accused. That's how you spot them. They yawn all the time and look over their shoulders. They can't stand still. These groups are much more preoccupied, up and down, scratch and rub, than the TV impersonators. The lawyers are sexier, impregnated with the actual. They've earned their black trappings. Heels and robes. They've heard it all: scandals and horrors, pitiful strategies, trajectories of fate. A cathedral of sanctioned lies. The greater your credit, your fiscal weight, the better the smokescreen. Language-bullies on a chessboard floor. It's not what you did, it's what you can afford. The time you can spare. The quality of the lunch served to the judge, the night he had.

The advocate George Carman - Thorpe's saviour, Aitken's nemesis - came directly to court from a gaming club. Done his wad, so they said. Elbow to elbow in a Soho dive with Frankie Fraser. Smoke-rinse hair, change of shirt. Cranked up for the performance he had to deliver, gone in the eyes. The remorseless interrogation of a man who has lost his soul.

Our case isn't being heard among the marble halls; it's in a remote satellite, the Thomas More Building. US style, without the cameras. An office, benches facing high table. A processing department for minor offenders, moral casualties.

The Clerk of the Court has a ruddy walnut tan, like furniture in a seaside showroom. 'Barbados is beautiful this time of year.' The lesser officials, runners, fetchers and door-openers, feed him his lines. A bag carrier makes the necessary response: 'You sod.' Collusive laughter. His skin, on closer examination (we have nothing else to do), is yellow, tight, health as hazard; nicotine pallor of beach-bar jaundice, drinks with straws sucked from chopped pineapples.

'Retire?'

'I'll finish my sentence.'

Caribbean Christmas. An offensively brilliant yellow silk tie boasts of ingested sunlight, surplus liquidity. It's metallic in its sheen, right in your face. The money shot in a porn movie. The Clerk's tie is an uncanny anticipation of New Labour's latest 'blue sky' thinking, its summer 2002 neckware directive. A terminal makeover for a tired administration, Euro-splash for conferences in Spain. The antidote to steely bureaucrats who have just been found out. A rethink on polished metal-rim specs, minimalist mouths. Jack Straw and the shamed Stephen Byers. Big ties! Feminine colours, pinks and yellows. A tasteful cough of Tabasco down your shirtfront. Something significant to take attention away from the dark rings under Piety Blair's armpits. A return to the lyric. Away from control freak knots and blade-thin tie strips. Tate Modern gestures of sponsored optimism. Ties for demi-gangsters, style bandits. Powerful men with big, soft, caring cocks.

Hands on the bench. Masonic rings. These characters hang around the courts and do the business before the lawyers, the functionaries and the judges appear. They're like smalltime betting-shop hoods, on the counter, out front, taking heat from whatever is going on in the backroom. They make their own rules. And they have only one law to obey: *get in early*. Be here. Keep out the riffraff. Round up reluctant clients of the system, the ones lost in the corridors.

At first, we're on our own. Sitting at the back, heads down. It's a day out, after a long winter. None of the accused, standing in bankruptcy, without hope of discharge, appear. But, at the very last moment, hesitant, unable to open the door without assistance, bottom-feeders creep to their pens. Self-advertising victims of a cruel system. No big ties, no ties at all. An Indian couple. A large black man who has been discovered, lurking. He won't give his name, but is persuaded to make up the numbers. A Chinese gentleman in grey suit and white shirt.

Green walls and blue, cloth-backed chairs. A purposefully indeterminate carpet. No footfalls to be heard. The room is detached from the forward motion of London, a limbo cell. The judge, bustling in, looks like Jonathan Meades with a humour bypass. The surface of the smooth bench, on which we lean, is pale, compressed veneer.

The prosecutors, bored, between appointments, go through the motions. Bundles of paper, ribboned folders, reams of documentation to outline: nothing. One set, it is clear, outballasts all the others. Two benches and three porters are required for Michael John Moorcock's green box files. A library of claims and counter-claims. Jarndyce vs. Jarndyce has nothing on this, tight-lipped amateurs. Mad rhetoric on a Russian scale. Generous in everything he undertakes, the man in the stetson has swamped his accusers with existential fictions, excesses of politesse, secure-ward courtesies. He has actually - and this is unforgivable - *answered their questions*. At length. In detail. With amusing asides, anecdotes, parentheses. He talks to them as if they were sitting on the other side of the table in the Overseas League. There are holograph revisions, firstsecondthirdfourth drafts, salvoes, satires, hand-drawn caricatures, diagrams, inserts, scripts printed on the reverse of rejected contributions to *New Worlds*.

But they take their revenge. Time means nothing to them. They will pursue Michael John Moorcock across oceans and deserts, deep into the deadlands. They are crazier than Charlton Heston in *Major Dundee* (or out of it). Moorcock, being part-Jewish, is a Hollywood Apache. They want his head.

The lawyers shape their performance to the mood of the judge. They speed up or slow down, according to the slightest droop of his eyelids, twitch of his hand. The belly of the Meades impressionist is audibly rumbling. He's like the new Meades, the thin Meades, trapped inside the comfortable casing of the ex-foodie, language gourmet. Trapped in enforced silence. Allowed to nod or pass on.

And for the defence? Not much. A youthful Afro-Caribbean woman under instruction. One old-school hack. Difficulties with documentation. Any old paper picked up in the rush to get out of the office.

The bankrupts huddle at the back of the room, pretending that they're not there. Nothing to do with me, guv. Wrong man. Mistaken identity. I was just passing, heard voices, looked in.

'Mr Kenney isn't expected this morning. We understand he is living in the Irish Republic.'

Unavailable.

'Currently living in Ireland.'

Not present.

'We understand he is not expected, letter on file.'

Legions of the invisible, the scarpered. Buck passers with their collapsed scams, their hopeless schemes. Bailiffs dispatched to empty properties, ringing on disconnected bells.

'Currently resident in Australia. Unable to attend, due to illness.'

'Not seen for several weeks - residing in San Francisco.'

'Enquiries were made at 49, Sidmouth Road, Willesden - we understand he left for Sierra Leone some time ago.'

It is all so understated, pleasant. Question and response. A ritual. Names, excuses. The judge, the clerks, the lawyers. Massed documents. The Moorcock archive (which, speaking as a demented collector, looks very tasty). I keep my eye on the green boxes, in case a scrap of Moorcockiana falls out. The Bodleian - where the good Doctor Hinton went mad, trying to keep pace with deliveries from Colville Terrace or Blenheim Crescent - had to put the block on Moorcock ephemera, a landfill of manuscripts and correspondence that threatened to bury Oxford. No more packing cases, please, from Lost Pines, Texas. The libraries admit now, they made a mistake, taking a punt on New Wave sf. They should have limited themselves to Ballard. No carbons, no multiples with different titles. One story to stand for them all.

'A medical condition. I understand we will receive a medical certificate. But it had not been received when I left the office this morning.'

He speaks, the judge.

'Very well, I'll stand it over.'

One of the unfortunates they have netted agrees to swear, on the Gita. He is asked about when he is willing to 'come in'.

'21 days,' says the prosecutor.

'60,' revises the bankrupt.

The judge settles for 28.

The wife of this sinner, an innocent party who put her name on the papers, is held to be equally culpable. She shakes her head, mutters. The Khans and the Kellys. The judge has done with them for today.

'Mr Moorcock isn't expected. Now resident in America. The matter will be adjourned until the 2nd of March.'

Pre-Ides. Time enough for Mr Moorcock to construct new rafts of correspondence. It has been, this fine morning, a kind of holiday. For us. Away from the desk. A false spring. We're free to cross that wide road, towards Senate House, pictures in heavy frames, the Impressionists and their river. We'll have to report back, it's true. Tell the man how it went. They've got his name in the book. He is now included in the role call of offenders. He's not forgotten.

ICHOR IS THE TRUE INK

through the long night at 20 minute intervals
the cry of car alarms rhythms
of sleep broken at the old desk
catching up with unnecessary paperwork
mewing cat songs the non-urgent penetration of
tired masonry, small yell, mechanical climax
appreciated by your unwitting correspondent

ANGELS OF CHANCE

*'poetry and geometry meet amidst these landscapes whose
greyness is as charged and nuanced as the sky before thunder'*
Raymond Durgnat

unhandled dogs waiting to be milked she digs

weevils out of a crack that runs down her thigh

murder fluff retrieved from broken nail

food on an oval plate an indelible photograph

quick-ink colours the tongue with false optimism

curtains double as nightdresses (negative weddings)

entry tickets to the 4th Dimension conferred on

those who have already vanished written out

the airhead who quits his station with a handful

of brown change purchasing a newspaper he

really doesn't want *this this this* is the ghosted

autobiography I refuse to acknowledge

SIX DANCERS MISSING

'It's an established fact, isn't it, Mr Bell, that paranoid schizophrenics
hear better than us normal people. You know, higher frequencies,
like dogs.'
Clancy Sigal

'Atlee' is the missing balcony-hound called
to interrogate my proofs, they'll detonate
the Holly Street towers in March, Laburnam Court
quilts the lambent pretensions
of neighbourhood terraces, forcible evacuation,
just like the war, with teeth and cars: a yard &
a half of greasy stool passed in a Lawrence, Kansas,
convenience store, hickory truncheon
with which to silence poor Atlee's insistent yelp

so tuck indigent poets beneath knotted boards
& let film-makers reverse the sexual polarity
of uncounted kids, jug jug, you tight-mouthed
daws, accepting wages for lardy questionnaires
reading territory like a final demand, woof woof
no offence taken where none intended, we'll stick

EVERY EACH OF US

'their nature to mob and molest'

love of rain from the safety of indoors
Bishopsgate cell where
it doesn't shatter but hangs in air
like a kinder pollen, washing away
protective coats & films, grey uniforms
which also invoke as on sweaty afternoons
inappropriate rage, risked on a single hand

dress this tale of how we sheltered away
from spoiled electrics, random shootings
black on black, unconvinced commuters
sleepwalking between multistorey assignations,
faking it for salary, savage city showers
splashing through the leaking arcade
a perfect circle of rust on a tin table

OUT THERE

THE MAN WHO TAUGHT LATIN TO CATTLE

'as free of the suave as the pinguid'
Thomas Pynchon

If we accelerate across a shelf of powdered glass tomorrow
eyes moist with flood & airports lime avenue
viaducts under pink & white blossom, west
wind drawing wings from a lightgreen coat hysteria of
onwards and upwards how smoothly the route unfurls
annulling prior arrangements feigning significance
dew pond within tyre-shriek of the complex
junction... Newspaper wicks hang from our heels as
showers rinse friendly dust we transit
Benedictine wool into the map's stitched seam, tithe barn
captured by IT pirates surveillance stalks
perimeter fence dividing a lush cabbage field green
tracks lead directly to the river water in our socks,
Colne & Thames dispute the market floor Staines or
Ad Pontes birthplace of linoleum and Ali G the Amazon
dot co warehouse station of this morning's shamanic
screen bowman who knows being dead that smoke kills
himself replaced within 8 hours by turned corduroy
earth... And remember friends the Alamo is flagged as
shorthaul kip US security and German motors if you
pass under 30 bridges republican graffiti must give
way to the sexual imperative: *SPIRITS COCK*

LOST GERMAN SHEPHERD

Kyrie eleison (an Alconbury tape)
ravelling between spools
counters hagiographic froth St Diana
Burberry huntress colour-enhanced
spinning diamond heart: sun's moss
amber & away glutting on
'the soundtrack of a Sean Connery film'
Umberto Eco's medieval mystery
in the chill room on Glastonbury Tor

rocks crushed to aggregate air-
bags pointlessly inflated as Bill
Clinton's latest bouffant moon skids
in rearview mirror French monks

cellophane flowers wilt on the forecourt
Lost Highways metempsychosis stone
falcons silence painted cows in a private
park privilege of speech suspended &
already Evita hordes scab their knees
drag tongues across gritty sandbox

blind in white beams another place
melisma mood muzak / bitch of words

REPRODUCTION ACTORS

'faces confiscated from elsewhere'
Theodor Adorno

The cortege runs backwards from the underpass
a black stick ordered through the post
arriving in stiff brown paper as the Exxon Valdez slick
dyno-rods a flushed interior, colonic
irrigation on a global scale, drowning cities...
it's too many years, deckboards & rivulets, since
I dreamt of a half-raised arm
the catastrophe on Brighton beach that did for
Old Labour sodden kecks bringing out the small
boy in him the once-&-never leader split
skirts in leather court shoes how pleasantly
post-prandial collapsing balconies on the wedding-
cake as all good men settle to deep cigars brandied
corruptions call girls sent home... Time dogs
breathe through salt-smeared portholes the tide
is feudally quiescent tonight no economic migrants
the secret is out there and it doesn't change

BARDO BEACHPARTY

*'It seemed to me that the scenery was being
changed for a time, but only for a time'*
                              Fyodor Dostoyevsky

heaven fell that night the glorious fourth
stars like grains of sand cut your corn
sticking-plaster in bidet sandwich
blue too rich to taste make tracks
barefoot bride Ava contessa courtesan
black matador pants without
visible pantyline whatever became of
Stephen Boyd or the brusque German
with the schnapps habit & a liking for lace
under leather chaps not oiled nor dusky
chaps from the High Atlas submariners
agents of Marina when Warner Brothers
whitewash hoodlum hash Spanish
residuals manhandle pups & baby grands
tempest seashore with mandatory lemon
groves balled fist sweetened with lavender
drives into the belly of memory it couldn't
it shouldn't it didn't happen south of
the border no mutual extradition treaty
misty river: previously unknown Mediterranean

FLESH IS HAIR TOO

'madness at sea is not quite so worrying as fire or theft'
Thomas Pynchon

in the beach photographs there are no
present beards or clay pipes
obstacles to plasma news from the other side
the sea folds tarpaper gods & navigators
on star shift stepping briskly to stern
the watcher at the stove hat like a chimney
boat-jaw dragged on shingle crust
eaten by salt won't accept black-edged
telegrams: light is meat & weight & duty
blanched return extended families of
net-mending fisherfolk who knew
how to lounge & when to disappear
their feet dipped in vinegar
shag (spray)
grey curls
gallantly on promenade anchor chains &
paint ranks of blackest cannon

KILPEC

rabbits on the raft
vinegar-boards in spite of
marine terror priapic
ears corbels & curves blushing
sandstone as the hosta leaf
vulva is generously spread
verdigris incontinent shy hands
defer earth mound launches
a rabid craft on landwaves circle
the tower midge oak dish
crafty musicians at the skirt
of things score heat
kneeprint on deck brain cup
a blackbird disgorged from
the throat's narrow aperture
fleeced saints lead the dance
ecstatic anywhere but resolution

GLINTON SPIRE

'homeless at home and half gratified'
John Clare

out by the chain one of the last daughters of the prominent
farming families Titmans Vergettes Websters tracks her
past leading a younger self vivid as cowslip to revision
beside egg-&-cress signboard by lych gate
romancing one-sided love: *JC 1808 MARY*
and on a Dutch bridge over an English dyke
greyhair leisure slacks from Peterborough they embrace
parked vehicle the mildest autumn day as a dog
splashes after a stick its patron in all this contrived space
gabbles on mobile phone
2 cars one animal line of poplars
the slender spire busy road at margin repeat offence
a temperature the small poet never achieved
discovering workmen surveying a field for coming
eastcoast railway hedge torn out public trim
aware of ungathered beef lost in thickets eaten fame
a face that won't go out printed from generation
to generation in affectionate Xerox too still to be real
our walk hanging baskets mild as death
Northamptonshire running flat to the grey sea

THE LIGHTNING BALL

*'the soul, however, in metempsychosis, will inhabit other
bodies, be they animal or human, and some will return
full circle back to Heaven'*
                                Sally Spedding

The old gentleman is standing in his garden, a photograph. Stiff postcard of his father, bearded, sitting on a highbacked wooden chair, brought out for the occasion. Dead. The boy at his side, features unresolved, on this dark night. Pudding-basin cut. Kitchen. His mother. Coarse towel. Flinching. Arms folded, jacket leaking light. Browngold. He scrutinises the person brought here to record this moment. His father and his earlier, more ancient self.

The night is cold to the ground, the air damp. The old gentleman is underdressed. A neutral observer would have every reason to feel alarmed. Furniture, for the most part, gone; chopped into firewood. He sleeps in a greasy bag in front of the fire. The fire has died. The bath, advanced in its day, is black as coal. A scene illustrating spontaneous combustion.

There are also colour prints from a throwaway camera, bought at a petrol station. Concerned relatives, let in, are shocked (it is just as they had imagined): ninety years and thirty years alone. Topdressing of meat-grease on orderly rows of books. Bodydust, articulate smoke: saturated paper. The books, unburnt, aspire to the condition of peat. Fuel. They are heavily annotated, but unconsumed.

It's dark, night. But he pushes the darkness back. It opens before him. He feels for cracks and channels. Man and house understand one another. Neither could be described as being in 'the first flush', both were born on this ground. There were rumblings, out over the sea, he felt the first heavy spots of rain. No coat, no shoes.

The police find him, wandering. Without name or coherent narrative. And, being lucky, in a fortunate part of the world, he is taken in.

He told the story to a nurse.

–Do you know what a lightning ball is?

He didn't wait for the reply she didn't make. She was looking out of the window, down the road, two women talking by a privet hedge; a red car parked and a white van stopping outside another large, converted property.

–Lightning has been recorded in the form of, or giving the appearance of, a string of bright beads. Several authorities - Wilson, experimentally verified by Gott - see lightning balls as being associated in some way with this phenomenon. Explanations, the scientists admit, are unsatisfactory. The balls move slowly and are often distinguished as having a 'rosy' appearance.

She turned, poured him an orange drink, tidied the few objects on the bedside table.

–An electrical discharge in the form of a glowing white, or slightly pink ball: it came down our lane. Scorching narrow hedges, blossom. As it had been, as I remembered it, in childhood. Tarmac and pedestrian crossing and high kerbstones revoked. Lightning bowling like a hoop. An unusual but far from unique occurrence.

He knew: this was an intelligence, the manifestation of an intelligence in which he was somehow implicated. The approach of the lightning ball, though not controlled by him, was controllable, eccentric. It's trajectory was personal. It was meant. Its advance, burning and absorbing - without hurt - everything in its path. A fierce clarity. It challenged and redefined matter. But was itself immaterial. You saw it because it wasn't there. And, in this act, this seeing, you yourself became invisible, translated. Plural.

Over the scruffy grass, ground dug up by foxes, pecked over by rooks and magpies, over heavy, nightwet bushes, it floated towards him.

Now the rain, which had been beating down so remorselessly, mistaking this place for somewhere else, drenching him, stopped. Or became unimportant. The ball of white light was intelligence, the sum of it. Time, dirt, pain, the complex interrelation of objects and memories: suspended. That day, this chair. His father.

That's what he wanted the nurse, putting his book back into the drawer, brushing the sleeve of the unfamiliar jacket, to know. *There is no death.* No period. Between himself and his father, the photograph; both of them looking out, no temporal barrier; no younger or older, no argument.

A man, in darkness, pushing the lightning ball forward. And another, closer to the house, drawing it in. So that it hovered, swerved, played, spun. That is something. In this sober playfulness, something. An immaterial intelligence.

Years of. Books, words. Sticking to one place. Unmarried, childless. Last of the last. Photographs in a red tin, left in the house, taken away by the young women. The electrical and chemical discharges left by faces before photographs: how they come forward to shape an expression, to stand in the shadows.

He smiled, he knew. Hollow cheeks, fingers running over thin stubble. Send for a barber. He didn't know how to order a taxi. He understood. Movement as intelligence. Limited, fallible. To be told. In this way. This place.

–Yes dear. Yes. The nurse said. And later, without making any special effort to remember, she wondered who she would tell.

DEAD LETTER OFFICE
(UNCOLLECTED)

THE HANGING BEACH

when camera refused its circuits blown
by roads shrapnel-damaged & low grey
cherry drape Paisley shawl on razorwire
H flicker what does H mean the sea
still there but I was not permitted to witness
couldn't eat silver card in Bloomsbury greek
wife's coat collar adjusted by my hand in
old-fashioned lift / we're - *just* - in the movie
cage bar interrogation sound & how
much I live in that worldy wholeness of
presence alleviated by continual smooth
wearing & resetting of pebbles unwitnessed
beyond recording the pitch & throw used
knowledge blood garden children tables
mistaking the page pulse in both our skins
melancholy punishment better than forgotten

light

NO BONES

brightness swims in city shoal
& sooty moss fills the sockets
of winged skulls / dim is
still-light & never hushed footfall under
lash of leaf & thick fig canopy

beehive omphalos graved
in dry honey: 'like a watering
can, the shape' - or pattern of
scorched souls, *coc-coc-coo*

of plumpnecked pigeon birds
spattered uneven
slabs, high London plane
so grandly scabby

multiple occupation
of slender tomb, standing room only

Margaret Jones (37), Rees Thomas (53),
Edward Sherwood (53), William Blake (69),
Mary Hilton (62), James Greenfield (38),
Magdalen Collin (81) of Bethnal Green Road

one name recalled, a few Celtic weeds deposited
in the wrong bed. amen so long goodbye

PINE HALO

what is it with black cats & cemeteries
how they belong and we trespass
curious on vistas of inadequately disposed
statuary: twin portraits hanging at
my right shoulder poet novelist bruised
to deepen bond painted over
fixed by mouth that instant of
swift passage between formerly & now
almost so cats important to both men
messenger spirits with abrasive word
lives stripped a layer at each sighting
welcomed at the grave of Keats the cold steps
deserted temples of Kensal Green foliage
black cats of the city float in discriminate
woodland catch them breathless movement
in shock of light lucid aboriginal morning

BEFORE I LEFT THE RUE GRIMOIRE

light darts from out there not so very far
strikes the inner sea we hope
precise equivalent soundless & scaled down
cupped swash of *it's there the wind*
rotation of skull that's the attraction
like to like caking over dusty with bonedrip
the bowl's an extraordinary ordinary
thatch of cloud now layered pinkgold
rococo now Wagner all fake rhetoric of
transience: *your dart my jelly*
sound as it slurps closed lid you can't hear

ARREST KLEE

only accountants know poets
their jaws the alligator state
failing brightly the condition
of flaw against which we kick
and take train rides for epiphanies
even crazy men or word of Hastings
in the company of the late war dead
who no longer travel or speak

FOXTROT FATALITIES ON THE COAST ROAD

sticky droplets blood on paste
missing cluster missing broach
cruising charity, cut hand
no idea what to do to staunch tissue
smell of dead things pee stain plate from
locomotives' union casette *Mean Streets*
nightscene café by Van Gogh clothes
won't walk away contagious radio
'also petted a giraffe (who was later killed
by lightning after a freak summer storm)'

the final entry in the log of Jack Hawking
metatemporal physicist & abused cabin boy

BLAIR'S GRAVE
(2006)

BLAIR'S GRAVE

'This gibberish had the sound of a mind unravelling'
                                        Don DeLillo

monkeyheaded earthenware drinking vessel
clatterrattles at behest of the man who blows
bad wind, fabricated facemask
unbuilds ziggurat of denial
talks piety, sweat meniscus drying blue
'I want I want', no trust-
worthy rung on ladder, so shred it
believe what I say I say: *foul heart's straw*

II

your city will be underwater, fool
better so, intimate
sleeves rolled, eyes wild won't focus
everything swims, dirty glass
eyes for onions, software
coloured wire, bird substitutes
duck and swim through skin
you cough: words are broken plates

III

what would occur if the beard of Bill Griffiths
was appointed, asthmatic wheeze-
master, workboss, retired labour
overlord, in place of mendacity, warp-truth
headlamps: 'like a patch of daylight'
you command, distressed
distressed bears huddled like
evangelists: spectators on a melting shore

IV

hasty strings at evensong, forlorn questions
in Cherie orchard, cold finger's rectal probe
curl of pubic fleece the circumlocution
office offends dignity, he cannot
cut the mustard gas, cress bed on chalk
which prime minister delivered most sick
notes which fucked least in righteous
'countercompositional thrusts', cancelled kids

V

peppering belly with hurt food, waiting on
chequered cloth, entertainers named & shamed
ventriloquised paste, nothing to say becomes
nothing to do, so roll under floodtide
stacked capital in drowned sheds,
mortars lobbed at mud fort
will they be burgled at the back door
with pokers and nuclear shingle, pilgrim
caste badge: *poverty chic or obedience*

VI

most of the food we receive is sacked Kurd
'English-Turkish-Greek-Continental'
grand alliance united nations redgreen
display tomatoes peppers dates brown
onions oranges with stalks lottery sales
to locally poor cancer ward horseflesh
afternoons funding exchange rate un-
satisfied banks CCTV records: knife damage

VII

looks like a boatman up against the wall
seawall? pretty much so, grave blocks
of uneven size weight distribution, bareheaded
like the wool is missing & unsure how
to stand, right fist curled childish the other loose
in pocket, touches hair-flesh, beard on
wrong part of the head, turn it, the fire:
food, dance, the mystical, history, crime

VIII

summer barque studio storm
like fireflies the lantern'd boats far out
across the dark lake, oil rigs & prisons
staggers ape-gait through
electric showers, 3 years slumbering on
the banks of the Ocean, died in LA
car crash theme: reshot, recut
fever, malaria, bicycle, vamp
he picked his chauffeurs for their looks

IX

anyplace but Utah hard snow the things you do
all the time are the ones you forget Perugino
madonna postcard lying on blue cloth of
Blake book, we were dreaming
the nuns the Bardot girl
do it again beginning where we let
go and out of the box bursts
waterstorm to freeze the city's previously
unrevealed source: opium gum, stiff tongues

X

they comb the beach for scotsmen who can't swim
to Malaya through the bottom of a bottle
gangs fire alcove benches in excited monologue
sights in yellow telescope are
purely bad blame not be apportioned
individual purchasers of ethical coffee or lords
of conspicuous charity stepping from full-
bellied aircraft in dark glasses which they remove
for interviews, much water still tastes of sewage

XI

Gordon Brown plants a tree in Kenyan slum
we're not the *Mail* we could stretch to 600
in the Hotel North the monkey never dies
grey-city city of invisible rails no sky
chili dogs chase empty beer bottles
see you around Molly raincoat
rain neon spells bead the narrator is
dead cinched belt a world without news

XII

clouds rack the judge is silent low ceiling
an illusory flag a world-set of ghetto
archetypes, mammal miss & her jack-nerved
dealer, deal tarot nativity swords
I know that old boy he used to be a boxer
when chafing cares shall cool at last
otherwise he must live out in misery
lamentable time, bet the house, balk gloom

XIII

police ambulance air gunship plead
guilty to everything pleabargain swastika armband
bad son manacles in the interpreter's house
spike threatens carotid artery moslem radio flying
bodies dance in hot air nothing gives
fine wrist slap tapioca tube mum's relief
family name friend saw old man rushing from
a krugerrand bank with bags of hot loot
therefore he swet, and did quake for fear

XIV

if you can't open gates of death like a blown safe
on the low-way to Beckton problematic pilgrimage
stalls in warground aftermath air inside burns
portal a mocking quotation to labour caduceus
safer to try the role you could not fulfil and now
father's kinder breath puffs a shopping bag
rats worms wires replace blood no virtual will
lifts roof of strategic walk: alone, sneezing

XV

again caught against seafret we are invited
to pelt the old gentleman with mud, self-generated
if practicable, by handful, arab-celt-gypsy
in american clothing, soft on stiffening body
has known cold & cell, damage, eyes won't open
until there is something solid to view,
against empty traffic invitation to shoot
never never allow that impropriety: reproduction

XVI

wife slips window which other men saw
unglassed framework dried stone on which
sponsor's message resolves into fingerprint of god
painter of nocturnes, watercolours, glaze under
glaze, rectangle of river, one portal certainty
between non-verifiable external witness & inward
prompting anxiety of influence, pulpy red
fibres, polyps, sand: it's there & you know it

XVII

BEWARE THE SEA. IT HAS THE SMELL OF BLOOD, OR LIFE
or letter set at paper-hanging angle, painter
stepped bespectacled before wall of sea photos
sea-on-sea, & fear, paper will give way before
storm erupts, real water, overwhelming in dip &
crush IT FLOWS GENTLY THIS END if you
watch with eyes and let dogs swim in your place
I LIVE IN HOPE OF A BROADCAST he relents
drag-ash coal clinker WILL NEVER EVER RETURN

XVIII

life at sea is like Night like nothing but itself
vertical recall depth-surface slippage weight
some blue likely to run over chase down moon
stalk of blindness too stiff sits suited in
horrible chair dictaphone chalkstripe spectacles
beginning of nothing, withering into white
headless worm, cones rods, older than fish, red
is silver: unpublished novel too small to read

XIX

knock on wood Berlin summer 1892 attempted
to photograph the soul storm in the archipelago
clouds ambitious of becoming water blue petitions
clothe the woman across the table taps his tank
repines Formica daily tabloid crossword marriage
metal in our gut sings we detonate windows
it doesn't help the bus if you step into traffic
how close you have to come to register zero

XX

returned chalk to floating light in car park
rolled from bed to tethered mother moon
departs traindoor drawn into bowed pain
discharge shines on curved section of nailed egg
processed slacks bluff against understatement
memories compete for space at night you twitch
partdead Apolyon's candle blown: holed
tongue swallows best, black wormy bread

XXI

by Sarah collecting walnuts to harvest ink
read lens eyebrows carved in suet
you'll never be released she improvises
call your soul the odour of this windowless
chamber expecting prick of rosewater lift
core temperature experimental procedures split
twin the form of the bone is really similar
bone of Luz excuses a lifetime's fruitless search

XXII

fullrack wire-music watering can bullet
held by gravity of address travel business class
hireling peasant throws up his arms
what is staged is also real bought at price
from hyacinth garden like when the Iraq war
started I'm a Californian & I go outside
paint cactus trophy somebody
records what I say publishes that banality
impact cuts beef stops mimicry: a true fall

XXIII

modernist architect round specs
inking dull-eye stacks all sharpness
straight torture police in buttoned uniforms
german green makes the place seem gay
he reported not many Jews found
we saw Warsaw burn & Modlin being burnt
a stirring spectacle inherited wealth stain
liver spots Houston oilmen: no atonement, none

XXIV

educated at Edinburgh & in Holland ordained
minister of Athelstaneford he published in
1747 *The Grave* a didactic poem of the starred
graveyard school consisting of some 800 lines
blank verse celebrates the horrors of death
fractured soul or skate cold dish of Blake's
borrowed pilgrim clawing through walls of clay
tenement madness by suicide-mouth possessed

XXV

dollar bulk captures Mafia weather
Sicilian-American or Balkan Ukrainian Siberian Jew
long coats on the pier all of a piece
we will sink your laughter-curated cow talk
cows they *know* & the ritual of steppe death
necklace light fellates black shoes
'who's paying?' carefully they step ashore
craft heading out to redundant statuary

XXVI

let out hooks & eyes if dressing required
simulate slack love text one thing
image quite another, what's lost gives
lion winged boat the constant glare
who commissioned paper passing across
table in Switzerland, barber in latex
bodysuit shot 3 times, midway no way
sleep leaks & garbage is the final reason

AFTERWORDS

*Thus does the 'Necessary Angel' of the poetic arrive to save the
'Angel of History' from dying of melancholy in a suffocating
world of ruins.*
    Youssef Ishaghpour

*To narrow the subject down to the question of poetics, Taussig rules
out the idea (put forward by Lévi-Strauss, among others) that the
shaman's song amounts to an ordering of internal chaos, for the
song itself is unintelligible, 'part of a baroque mosaic of discourses
woven through stories, jokes, interjections, and hummings taking
place not only through and on top of one another during the actual
seance but after it as well.'*
    Anthony Mellors

*My favourite politician was Arizona Senator Barry Goldwater, who
reminded me of Tom Mix, and there wasn't any way to explain that
to anybody.*
    Bob Dylan

COMING TO THE CROSSROADS
(2006)

COMING TO THE CROSSROADS

You park in the middle of nowhere, letting the engine cool. Chill glass - the viewing panel in a coffin - fogs with warm breath, ticking metal. And the mess of memory begins to cook. You have been here before. Been everywhere in this part of the city, old London, no London, liminal land beside a working canal that no longer works. They have a laminated information board, fixed history, to let you know where you stand and what you should be thinking. Memory is pre-ordained, decided by professional explainers, edited by committees. It is sentimental, contrived. Like a movie by Spielberg (a man who gnaws hamburgers at 10 o'clock in the morning, room service), finessing pain into commodity. You crank a handle, the map speaks to you in the voice of Maud Winnington-Ingram, a parson's daughter, born in 1880. While you crank, she utters. When you stop, the voice dies. 'It's strange, my first encounter with the canal was...' The rest is lost, buried under the scream of bulldozers, earthmovers, welding guns.

I worked here in 1974. Spring, summer, autumn. In early winter they let the casuals go or found some excuse to dismiss them. I cut grass around the Hawksmoor churches - St Anne's, Limehouse; St George-in-the-East - and I spiked rubbish, picked up broken glass, the discarded sherry bottles of vagrant drinkers. (The rector could be found in the vanished pub, the Blade Bone. We shook keys from his waistcoat pocket, explored tower and crypt, spidery catacombs.) This warehouse building, viewed across a wilderness meadow, was busy with fork-lift trucks, palette boards, cans of dubious provenance; outdated meats for the shelves of cut-price minimarkets. Now sodium light blazes, prison style, on a football pitch, brilliantly green, a synthetic carpet. Shouts, movement. The pitch is dwarfed by a small municipal stadium which will soon be inflated to suit the requirements of the Olympic bid, the land piracy. The icicles of Docklands glint and flicker on the horizon. Money is another form of light. Touch it and it talks. Canary Wharf is the projected beam of a defunct cinema, a solid Xerox of De Mille pyramids and recycled bullion.

The show in the canalside warehouse is called *Antix*, a title revised by a spray-can bandit to *Anti-X*. Antichrist. Antichrist in Limehouse. 2,000 cubits from the crossroads. Do you know what a cubit is? 'An ancient linear unit based on the length of a forearm, from elbow to the tip of the middle finger.' But who walks on their arms? You have to take this measurement, an element of London's sacred geometry, on trust. Cubitt is also the name of a speculative builder. William Cubitt laid out the railway that linked Blackwall Dock and Tower Hill. He had his own settlement, his brand on the city, Cubitt Town at the south-east corner of the Isle of Dogs. Tower Hill was once the place of execution, for traitors and malcontents, preachers of false doctrine. Heads severed. A wall of eyes. The gazing mob freezes the moment when human heat is lost in a gush of blood. The place itself, just outside the bastion of the Tower, is earth heaped over the head of the Celtic giant, Bran. The myth of the founding of the city: a head, its eyes eternally open, watching the river. Ribbons of flesh attended by ravens.

All measurement starts from this site. Tower Hill is backed by the white stone of the old Port of London authority building, an angular Byzantine temple in which every ship coming up the Thames was recorded, nibs scratching on parchment. River gods, massive carvings of Neptune and his chariots, disguise a roof garden where marine insurance brokers take their meetings, power breakfasts; champagne and orange juice, buttery croissants.

Pressing through the heavy doors of the warehouse, I am invited to put my face to a padded tube that looks like one of those old (and dangerous) X-ray machines. Shards of coloured glass wink in an end-of-the-pier toy, the hum of bad electricity. Something is stolen from me, peeled away. My public face. The performance arena, hushed and dark, has been arranged to feel like a primitive chapel designed by Ikea. Too much cheap wood. The preacher, the man in black, has a board hung from his neck: a portrait. My face stolen from the tube and transmitted, a grinning skull. This story - our city - is all about heads. The man walks, a penitent, round and round the room, and my face, shifting, rolling, walks with him. His heels ring. His mad eyes shine. He breathes hard. You can see a chipped tooth held in his open mouth like a black penny.

Emanuel Swedenborg, a young man, twenty-two years old in 1710, takes passage from Göteborg to the port of London. A sorry sequence of annoyances, delays, mental trials. A bad novel. Plague warnings, quarantine: Wapping Old Stairs. He comes in on the tide like an ugly rumour. This sheep-head scientist, holy fool. Celibate enquirer. The youngest of the dead. A walking corpse with peach-fuzz on his cheeks. He hunts the soul to the innermost recesses of the body. Place is an undefined riverside geography. He is fetched. As they are all fetched, these madmen. They lay down memory traces in the clay of London. Reveries, visions.

Swedenborg, a talkative skull, is frantic to be buried alive. The spirits were deceitful. He saw what they saw; he saw through their eyes. A New Church, Jerusalem, must be made on this meadow: earthed, fitted with towers, lanterns, octagons, domes, urns. He was 'Samson shorn by the churches'.

Landfall.

The sour river fog is romance, future fiction. He slips ashore, a man forbidden. The plague-ship is tied up at Wapping Old Stairs, under a six week prohibition. He is caught. He should have been dosed with gin, hung in chains while three tides washed over him. He has privileged connections: Erik Benzelius, his brother-in-law, is a bishop. He is saved, condemned to live.

Emanuel has an 'immoderate desire' for knowledge, for the pressure of libraries, skills to master: lens grinding, clock-making, book binding. There are machines to develop or to invent: submarines, blast furnaces, fire extinguishers, maps of the human brain.

Conventional, shrewd, affable, damned: the young man was a fugitive in the streets, the close alleyways, the chasms between warehouses. That time in his life is expunged. From the instant he stepped ashore, time-traveller, he was in suspended motion.

What he discovered survives to this day, a wild orchard. A thatch of white blossom, a tangle of broken boughs: thorns, couch grass, berries. Between Cable Street and the Highway, to the south of Wellclose Square, a green tunnel. A grove sequestered from the open ground in which is buried the rubble of the Swedish Church, Ulrica Eleonora. Persistent exploration locates a grey stone font on which the church is depicted as a black ark, a hostage to the furies.

Swedenborg was buried in a vault beneath this altar. In 1908 his body was exhumed and returned to Uppsala; out once more upon the river. The skull, so it is rumoured, was mislaid. Does it wink beneath the bar of the sewerman's pub, the Crown & Dolphin, with other contraband trophies: the caput of John Williams (De Quincey's Ratcliffe Highway murderer), defaulting gangsters, the bone lanterns of the London disappeared? Or was the pillaged head fated to become a Masonic resource, boxed in black velvet in the depths of Queen Street?

The boy, the stranger, lies on coarse grass. His back rests against a gnarled tree. Dappled sunlight. Shadowplay on white, outstretched hands. Swedenborg's soul is resolved into discrete points of motion. It is of one substance with the sun. He is diffused, lost, estranged from himself. No longer does he converse with the dead. He died, here, and became one of them. He remembered what was not yet known. Then he raised himself up, brushed his long jacket, walked away.

In the city of the lost - missing skulls, heads wrapped in newspaper - they laboured to erase all memory of Swedenborg's transit. William Blake challenged him, recognised his spirit. Two-thousand cubits from Tower Hill to the demolished Wellclose Square. To the crossroads where they buried John Williams, head removed, stake through the heart. Swedenborg Gardens: a block of deadpan, East European housing, occupied by termites, invisibles. Wellclose Square has a suspended history of alchemists, seekers, visionaries, quacks: the Kabbalist Chaim Jacob Samuel Falk, maker of golems, collector of Thames mud. When the ceremony had been completed - oil of eggs, wax, amber, sage, cloves, tartar - Swedenborg appeared, celestial messenger. A northern golem of moonlight and dust. The confirmation of Falk's instinct: that he could raise the dead.

Emanuel is staying at the King's Arms, which is managed by a fellow Swede, Erik Bergström. Bergström keeps a journal. His paying guest, so he reports, dresses in velvet, breakfasts on black coffee, walks out every morning. The diary does not mention the visit to Falk. There were unrecorded discussions, scholars conclude, on Kabbalistic sexual techniques, orgasms achieved by meditation on the letters of the Hebrew alphabet. Forgotten knowledge. Swedenborg builds a clock for accurately calculating time at sea (where there is no time). He comes to the crossroads, Cannon Street Road, Cable Street. (All the shops here are packed with naked and headless mannequins. The heads have been turned to stone and arranged, in relief, above doorways. Tell the demons to pass on.)

From the west, down Cable Street, march the defeated blackshirts, kept out by barriers of furniture, upended vehicles. From the river, we anticipate Swedenborg. From the east comes an uncertain future, Thames Gateway; a virtual city with no soul, no memory. From the north, at last, comes the gentleman in black, the one all London writers acknowledge. Christopher Marlowe, Oscar Wilde, Rimbaud. The Faustian contract: fame, a hot coal on the tongue, silence.

In the now deserted warehouse, beside the canal, our conjuror - a music hall ghost, Tommy Cooper possessed by Joseph Beuys - unveils the prophetic head. Friar Bacon constructed a head of brass and coaxed it to language. The performance artist, in a dumb time, draws back his cloth of gold to reveal a head carved from industrial sausage meat. He digs at it with dirty fingers and offers scraps to the invisibles, the silent ones. The unrequired witnesses.

The head is free to speak, muddy obstructions cleared. The mouth is all word, lips quiver. This marvellous trophy is exhibited behind the closed doors of East End pubs: the Crown & Dolphin, the Old Horns, the Carpenters' Arms, the Seven Stars, the Grave Maurice. Smoked pink in the flame of igniting cigars, dead talk. The episode that is and was Emanuel Swedenborg will never be concluded, not here, not until the word, whose ghost he is, has been spoken. Now and forever. The London writer is incapable of expressing his meaning, or escaping from it.

Swedenborg is immune to the touch of the wind. If he comes into contact with even so much as the shadow of a dog, he is lost. A star burnt in quicklime.

I dip, at random, into a book of emblems published in 1869. A letter from Mrs Butler (Fanny Kemble) is quoted: 'What, for instance, is more beautifully suggestive of time than the perpetual rolling of a river? The Swedenborgians consider water, when the mention of it occurs in the Bible, as typical of truth.

I love to think of that when I look at it, so bright, so pure, so transparent, so temperate, so fit an emblem for the spiritual element in which our souls should bathe and be strengthened - from which they should drink and be refreshed.'

ACKNOWLEDGEMENTS

Fluxions (1983) was originally published as an Albion Drive Chapbook in an edition of 21 copies.

Flesh Eggs & Scalp Metal (1983) was published as a Hoarse Commerce Chapbook in an edition of 12 copies.

Autistic Poses (1985) was published by Hoarse Commerce in an edition of 10 copies.

Significant Wreckage (1988) was published by Words Press, Childe Okeford, Dorset, in an edition of 200 copies. My thanks to Julian Nangle.

Jack Elam's Other Eye (1991) was published by Hoarse Comerz in an edition of 200 copies.

Penguin Modern Poets 10 (1996) included work by Douglas Oliver and Denise Riley. My thanks to Tony Lacey at Penguin.

The Ebbing of the Kraft (1997) was published by Equipage, Cambridge. My thanks to Rod Mengham.

White Goods (2002) was published by Goldmark, Uppingham. My thanks to Mike Goldmark. And to my collaborator, Emma Matthews.

Saddling the Rabbit (2002) was published by etruscan books, Buckfastleigh. My thanks to Nicholas Johnson.

'Blair's Grave' (2006) is part of the collection *Buried At Sea*, published by Worple Press, Tonbridge. My thanks to Peter and Amanda Carpenter.

The first version of *Walking Up Walls* was issued as a card-concertina, by Agnew's of Old Bond Street (2001), to accompany reproductions of paintings by Jock McFadyen.

Coming to the Crossroads first appeared in *Stockholm New Music: Place and Space*. Stockholm, 2006. My thanks to Magnus Hagland.

I should like to thank Nick Austin and John Muckle of Paladin for bringing out *Flesh Eggs & Scalp Metal: Selected Poems 1970-1987*, a book which contains earlier versions of some of the texts published here.

Colin Still of Optic Nerve (in conjunction with Birkbeck) produced a spoken-word CD called *Dead Letter Office (Poems 1970-2004)*. Some of the texts in the present collection are performed, alongside others from an earlier period. The CD is part of a series distributed by Carcanet.

Dedication:

This selection is for the two Roberts, Bond and Sheppard. Who were prepared, hands dirty, to stir the original soup.

Index of titles and first lines

(1) ¹/₂ the pickled brain of Wyndham Lewis   153

1. On a ridge above the Dartford Crossing, the   213

¹/₄ inch to the W. of   87

14 DIE IN TREE FEUD   78

7 hours sealed, hurtling or snoring   52

A BULL CALLED REMORSE   53

A crimson mouth smirks in his frosty forehead   172

A FEW HUNDRED YARDS FROM THE DWELLING OF MR PRYNNE   57

A GROUP OF MEN, ALL CALLED JOHN   136

A HANDSHAKE ON THE TELEPHONE   35

A HAT THROWN IN THE AIR, A LEG THAT'S LOST   63

a lightgreen coat moves commonly east, un-   224

a man can fall backwards from a window   145

A PAINTER CALLED MILTON   228

A SERIOUS OF PHOTOGRAPHS (RIVERWALK FROM THE ISLE OF GRAIN TO OXFORD)   186

A SUITCASE CALLED ANTLER   42

a warren of secrets   61

above / darkened water, above the...   24

ADDITIONAL AGENTS   182

'Ain't got much expenses,' Eddie said. Man without expenses is nothing.   81

always the muff, mouth agape   41

Among stone ear fractures night   200

among the unfumigated lungs of the poor   110

an excitement of too much   60

AN IRISH NOVELLA   76

an old man cycling   70

an unclarified moon bounces   78

An unequal contest. 12th January, 2001. Royal Courts of Justice. Regina vs.   229

ANGELS OF CHANCE   172

ANGELS OF CHANCE   235

aniline dye travels faster than my will permits   106

APPROACHING OUNDLE BY ROAD   27

ARREST KLEE   257

As in a story...   18

as old men dancing return sap to springboard   139
as the circuit of the garden is an oval sentence   115
as to the clinker'd heart -   79
as unlikely as 'Canadian Pataphysics'   54
'Atlee' is the missing balcony-hound called   236
atrophy of idiolect   151
AUTISTIC POSES   74
BARDO BEACHPARTY   243
BATTERIES OR WHISKY   50
BECKTON ALP   201
BEFORE I LEFT THE RUE GRIMOIRE   256
BELHAVEN   168
better wander the town   133
BIG FACE, SMALL RAZOR   55
bird-creole or the billowing froth of bridesong   175
BLAIR'S GRAVE   263
BLIND MENDOZA'S TALLOW SAUCER   144
BOAT DRESSES   118
'boiled cabbage & gin hanging in the air'   134
BREATHING IS THE SAME METHOD AS DROWNING   112
breathless on that incline   84
brightness swims in city shoal   254
BUNHILL FIELDS   152
BUSINESS LOVE   220
CAMERA OBSCURA (OXFORD)   119
CASTING DEVILS AS SHELLFISH   47
celebrate the loss of rain   141
CHERNOBYL PRIESTS   111
chill Pils in Oxo / heady as   181
CHINESE BOXES   215
cinema flag (on clean white pole   140
climbing sun boulders the hillcrest   28
Cocteau directing   82
comestible sunlight refined by the cherry tree's pink   154
COMING TO THE CROSSROADS   281
CONTINUOUS SKY   224
CRAZY AS IN RAZOR   103
CROSSING THE MORNING (VALE CRUCIS)   28
CRYING, LIFE! LIFE! (TOWARDS BEDFORD)   29
Cycle with Jock and hear the past told. Pylons gates cemeteries under a big sky.   201

Dartington territory, fine bright air   26
day special so ordinary plain birds   197
DEGAUSSING THE WOLFMAN   160
DELETED, NOT DESTROYED   166
DETAILED DESCRIPTION OF A HOMOSEXUAL ACT   83
DIRTY DANCING AT THE ROEBUCK   147
Discretions of Chelsea, barrack grass no goats   179
Doctor Syenite had a book in which the names of the living had been printed.   128
DOCTRINE OF VARNISHED MORTAR   30
DROWNED FIELDS (WHITECHAPEL)   21
dusted in unexceptional manuscripts   63
DYNASTY = NASTY YAWN   79
earlier when   42
EGG ROLLING IN A STONE AGE CULTURE   151
either nude and shoved behind as well as   53
ENTERING COLIN COUNTRY (BEYOND STAMFORD)   22
escape with the children but   89
EVERY EACH OF US   237
Fire or an angled wind   21
fixed fallen folded / dereliction   58
FLESH EGGS (TRELIGGA)   56
FLESH IS HAIR TOO   244
FLUXIONS (LINCOLN)   18
fly by night   204
folded children   199
fording pondlife to pamper your Arab steed   162
Fournier Street, dusk is absolute, outside   221
FOXTROT FATALITIES ON THE COAST ROAD   258
FRIENDLY FIRE   133
FROM THE THICK END OF A PURFLEET TELESCOPE   206
furze warmed   29
GAUDY LIVERS   221
GERMAN BITE   60
GIN HAD NO CONNECTION WITH TIME   113
GLIBBERY ELECTRICAL   149
GLINTON SPIRE   246
GOOD ICE: DO NOT ENTER THROUGH RUBBER DOORS   81
GUIGNOL'S BAND AID   199
HALF OF PLUS (DURHAM)   164
hang-loose journos decant stateside w/cash   148

hard on the heels of hope, westwards   186

hearing the approach of fish   22

heaven fell that night the glorious fourth   243

HENCE, LIKE FOXES   54

her heels worn raw   74

here and there   27

his bare arm, a gold box   69

HOME OF THE TONG, OR THE DREAM-DETECTIVE   51

horn of plenty with bayonet warmth   182

HOW THE MESSAGE WAS BROUGHT   128

HURRICANE DRUMMERS SELF-AID IN HAGGERSTON   85

I   127

iceblue shoulderbands against wetpink door   149

ICHOR IS THE TRUE INK   234

if the cat has your name and dies   35

If we accelerate across a shelf of powdered glass tomorrow   240

IMMACULATE CORRUPTIONS   134

in Boston (Lincs) / a last cigar   88

in late sky sheep float   205

in Madison the squares   80

in midair shifting gravity to open doors   47

In oyster bars / shells   144

in the beach photographs there are no   244

IN THE LATEST PROOF OF ACKROYD   87

In Victoria's Park...   50

inside: sheep   51

INSOMNIA   145

IRE-BOUND HOSE CO   173

is the yellow twin on a straight country road   160

It was the doctor, one of them, one of those Jacks they talk so much about.   125

JACK ELAM'S OTHER EYE   101

keys swinging he comes   83

KILPEC   245

KITING THE FLIES   41

KRISTALLNACHT   89

Kyrie eleison (an Alconbury tape)   241

LA RAGE (PENZANCE)   52

LANDSCHAFT (OXFORD)   165

Last night the witch came to me offering lampreys on iron,   173

late daisies, burnt leaves   105

leaves heavy as shed skin   142

Lepidopterist of memory. Of ice-erasure. The road.   119

let crows with their cutpurse habits   143

letter never sent, of things you didn't see   101

light darts from out there not so very far   256

Like a butcher I relish the drive to work   146

LOST GERMAN SHEPHERD   241

love of rain from the safety of indoors   237

LOWESTOFT TWINNED WITH PLAISIR   70

MALDOR FURS   109

mid-afternoon / lazy bars   136

midnight daughters splice the lemon summons   109

monkeyheaded earthenware drinking vessel   263

MORE AMOROUS THAN IMAGINATIVE   59

more diseases than textbooks   75

MORE KISSING THAN TEACHING   140

MORE SPIT THAN POLISH   181

MORPHIC RESONANCE   31

MR MOORCOCK IS NOT EXPECTED   229

MULLET GARDENS   161

NEARLY A MOON   169

Nether Stowey / to Highgate   30

NICE BLOOD   205

NIL BY MOUTH   110

NO BONES   254

no camera gun so the rain slides unthinking   165

no lounger to challenge the sea's reality   169

NOSTALGIA IS A WEAPON LIKE THE BLISS OF PETER RACHMAN   61

OBSCENERY OF THE EAST   198

OCEAN ESTATE   162

Once blueblack Velcro supported a wounded knee   180

only accountants know poets   257

Ophitic spit: mention another   20

opposite the scrapyard & across the river   104

OTHERING THE ANGELS   154

out by the chain one of the last daughters of the prominent   246

out of the cloister the poetry reading fugitive faces   113

PARADISE ROW   148

PARROT TAROT   203

peel the onion sky over Purfleet black   212

PINE HALO   255

POGROM MUSIC   106

POST-RABBINICAL SLUMBERS   58

PRECIOUS & STRAW   137

    prize cicatrix in oil suspension   150

PULHAMITE GROTTO IN SILVERTOWN   200

    rabbits on the raft   245

RADIO STRUMPETS   40

    rain is a solid / seal the cupboard   203

RAISING THE GOLEM   125

    rasp with tongue the belly of an old wristwatch   168

    razor sex white as memory debate   112

READ MY LISP   143

    receipt the work of a life uncorrected proof   228

RECOVERY & DEATH   105

RED HAIR, LIKE A SPIDER GLUTTED ON IRON   19

REPRODUCTION ACTORS   242

RE-READING ROTHSCHILD'S LAPWING   39

REVENGE OF THE RIVER HORSE   141

REVENGE, LAUGHTER, PARADISE   174

ROOM SERVICE DECLINED   222

ROUGH TRADES (OAKHAM)   15

    running into wind that tunnels a fist   102

SANCTUARY KNOCKER   135

    Saved in salt, face partially crushed & drooping eye   174

SCARPS & GREEN HEAPS   104

    seaweed luxury bath essence   55

SERPENT TO ZYMURGY   75

SERPENT'S TAIL TATTOO COMPULSORY   179

'SERVED CLUMSILY' (TOTNES)   26

    Shadows across the desk were obtrusively dense, the detail too interesting   76

    Shadows of hammer-headed daffodils yolk mismatched stripes of human   161

SIGNIFICANT WRECKAGE   93

SIX DANCERS MISSING   236

SLOOZE   212

    smalltown mid-land   15

SNAPSHOTS FOR ROBINSON (DARTFORD TO GRAVESEND)   213

SNOW LIP   175

    So much can be said when walls are left   147

SOLITARY AFFRAYS   108

some things the same   39
SOS: CARFAX   211
spent in / Lamian transactions   19
SPIRIT LEVELS   48
sticky droplets blood on paste   258
STREET DETAIL   69
SUB (NOT USED): MOUNTAIN   150
sweating bread & Colombian coffee   138
TACKY ADMIRALS   88
talking of the Sheik, his rivers of blood speech   71
TALKING WITH CAROLYN   63
tanking in behind screams the   72
Tell them to take off the strait-waistcoat. I have had a terrible dream.   206
THAT WHICH APPEARS   139
the audience is a Jew & the Audience is not   103
The brokering of secret spaces. Poets haunt the purlieus of the city in direct   222
THE CARNAL GATE: HITMAN IN PRIVATE GARDEN (LAMB HOUSE, RYE)   115
The cortege runs backwards from the underpass   242
the director sniffing yellow   215
THE DOUBLE'S DOUBLE   123
THE EBBING OF THE KRAFT   146
the epic which is a tractor   16
THE EXHIBITION I DIDN'T HOLD AT THE TATE WOULD HAVE INCLUDED   153
THE FALLS (TALGARTH)   17
THE FIFTH QUARTER   180
the figure of the messenger   37
THE GLAMOUR'S OFF   16
THE HANGING BEACH   253
The hills above Port Glasgow   48
THE KONIGSBERG BRIDGE PROBLEM   204
THE LIGHTNING BALL   247
THE MAN WHO TAUGHT LATIN TO CATTLE   240
The old gentleman is standing in his garden, a photograph. Stiff postcard of   247
the old woman who talks to birds   108
The performance artist is criminal, one of the privileged of the city.   166
the proximate fig shades a shale envelope   152
THE SHAMAN'S POUCH (MANISH, ISLE OF HARRIS)   117
the small (wooden)   211
the telephone rests on Swedenborg Yeats too &   135
The Turk sent his catamite swimming to shore   93

there is death in us we are all sick &   111

there was a man set to dig a stone   59

There were no mirrors in the attic, the investigator said. And not much light   123

There's a mob of rumours from s. of the river   85

THERMOMETERS OF THE DAMNED   102

THOSE TIMES   82

through the long night at 20 minute intervals   234

TO WHOM IT MAY CONCERN   72

tonight, albumen, the moon   40

TRAVELLERS BY APPOINTMENT ONLY   142

TRAVELLING IN SPITE STOCKINGS   9

trust is a meadow the light in my eyes   63

under slow-flume   57

under the castle's ox / red stone   164

unhandled dogs waiting to be milked she digs   235

unyielding, the pliancy of   117

Walking through wet wheat an ocean of mercury after   177

walking to where there is no weather   198

WALKING UP WALLS   193

WARD BONDAGE   71

wasps mate with shadows,   31

wax elephants of Whitechapel   220

we are not given many and do not realise   17

WHARF WHARF   80

what is it with black cats & cemeteries   255

WHAT THE HERMIT WROTE IN HIS DIARY   127

when camera refused its circuits blown   253

WHERE THE TALENT IS   138

whisky & flakes of green leaf,   118

whistle of the cat-catcher in the night   137

WHITE AIR   37

WHITE GOODS   197

white herm: a cyclone   56

Woke up this morning.   193

WORLD'S OLDEST COMEDIAN IS DEAD   177

WRITTEN AT ATTENTION, TO THE SOUND OF RUNNING WATER   20

XENOMANIA, THE ROAD   24

You park in the middle of nowhere, letting the engine cool. Chill glass   281

YOU SAW 5 SUNSETS IN 4 DAYS   84

Twenty-six copies of *The Firewall* are cased and lettered A-Z by the author and contain an additional handwritten text. A further twenty-six copies are cased, numbered and signed: these contain an additional phrase.

Fifteen Roman numbered copies are *hors commerce.*

9 october 2005

—

I climb for a cooling sea
to sit on low concrete shelf

' You'll live forever,' the woman says,
' but why, darling, why ?'

Iain Sinclair

' V '